# the golden triangle

# the golden triangle

## an ethno-semiotic tour of present-day India

## Arthur Asa Berger

Taylor & Francis Group

LONDON AND NEW YORK

First published 2008 by Transaction Publishers

Published 2017 by Routledge
2 Park Square, Milton Park, Abingdon, Oxon OX14 4RN
711 Third Avenue, New York, NY 10017, USA

*Routledge is an imprint of the Taylor & Francis Group, an informa business*

Copyright © 2008 by Taylor & Francis.

All rights reserved. No part of this book may be reprinted or reproduced or utilised in any form or by any electronic, mechanical, or other means, now known or hereafter invented, including photocopying and recording, or in any information storage or retrieval system, without permission in writing from the publishers.

Notice:
Product or corporate names may be trademarks or registered trademarks, and are used only for identification and explanation without intent to infringe.

Library of Congress Catalog Number: 2007048941

Library of Congress Cataloging-in-Publication Data
Berger, Arthur Asa, 1933-

    The golden triangle : an ethno-semiotic tour of present-day India / Arthur Asa Berger.
      p. cm.
    Includes bibliographical references and index.
    ISBN 978-1-4128-0787-6
      1. Rajasthan (India)--Description and travel. 2. Tourism--Social aspects--India--Rajasthan. I. Title.

DS485.R2B38 2008
302.20954'4--dc22

                                                                         2007048941

ISBN 13: 978-1-4128-0787-6 (pbk)

For Kaye S. Chon

*No state in India is as rich in magnificent palaces and forts, colourful festivals and bazaars, as Rajasthan. Stretching 342,000 sq. km (132, 047 sq miles), the state is bisected by the Aravalli Range, which runs diagonally from the northeast to the southwest. Its main river is the Chambali. The Thar Desert, which covers western Rajasthan, was once ruled by three great kingdoms—Jaisalmer, Jodhpur, and Bikaner. Shekhwati, with its painted* havelis, *is in the semi-arid north while the eastern plains have the bustling state capital, Jaipur, and the Ranthambore National Park, famous for its tigers.*

—DK Eyewitness Travel Guides, *India*

# Contents

| | |
|---|---|
| Foreword | xi |
| Preface | xv |
| Acknowledgments | xix |

**Part 1: Rajasthan as a Tourist Destination—An Analytic Perspective**

| | |
|---|---|
| 1. Tourism in India and Rajasthan | 3 |
| 2. Tours and Tourists in Rajasthan | 17 |
| 3. Hierarchical India and Egalitarian America | 27 |
| 4. Grid-Group Tourism and India | 31 |

**Part 2: Semiotic Rajasthan**

| | |
|---|---|
| 5. Semiotics and Tourism | 41 |
| 6. A Semiotic Perspective of Rajasthan (and the Golden Triangle) | 47 |

**Part 3: Rajasthan Remembered**

| | |
|---|---|
| 7. Remembering Rajasthan | 81 |
| Bibliography | 99 |
| Index | 101 |

# Foreword

*India has few important towns. India is the country, fields, fields, then hills, jungle, hills and more fields. The branch line stops, the road is only practicable for cars to a point, the bullock-carts lumber down the side tracks, paths fray out into the cultivation and disappear near a splash of red paint. How can the mind take hold of such a country? Generations of invaders have tried, but they remain in exile. The important towns they build are only retreats, their quarrels the malaise of men who cannot find their way home. India knows of their trouble.*
—E. M. Forster, *A Passage to India*

## Researching Rajasthan

This volume is not a traditional guidebook to Rajasthan offering lists of good hotels and restaurants, along with information about cities and sites of interest. It is, instead, an ethnographic and socio-semiotic study of Rajasthan culture. But since it deals with many of the most important tourist sites and aspects of culture in Rajasthan that are of interest to tourists, it will considerably enhance the experience of anyone visiting "The Golden Triangle" and Rajasthan. So I like to think that it is a tourism guide in a more profound sense of the term "guide."

Many people are not familiar with the terms "semiotics" and "ethnography," so let me say something briefly about ethnography here. I will discuss semiotics later in the book.

## Ethnographic Analysis

Ethnography is a form of social science research that uses participant observation as the basic means of understanding whatever is being studied. It is a form of research in which the experiences of the researcher play an important role and are the basis for whatever conclusions the researcher makes. The term ethnography means, literally speaking, "a picture" (*graphy*) of a people (*ethnos*). So this book is based on my experiences in Rajasthan and my interpretations of these experiences.

In his classic work, *Tristes Tropiques*, the great anthropologist Claude Lévi-Strauss explains how he suddenly came to recognize the importance of ethnographic analysis. He writes (1970):

> It may seem strange that I should so long have remained deaf to a message which had after all been transmitted for me ever since I first began to read philosophy, by the masters of the French school of sociology. The revelation did not come to me, as a matter of fact, till 1933 or 1934 when I came upon a book which was already by no means new: Robert H. Lowie's *Primitive Society*. But instead of notions borrowed from books and at once metamorphosed into philosophical concepts I was confronted with an account of first-hand experience. The observer, moreover, had been so committed as to keep intact the full meaning of his experience. (pp. 62-63)

First-hand experience and observation, then, is the basis of ethnographic research—a methodology commonly employed by anthropologists and other kinds of social scientists. And this book contains my firsthand experiences in "The Golden Triangle" and Rajasthan, which are often tied to, and supported by, insights by historians and other kinds of scholars about Rajasthan and India.

## The Design of the Book

The first part of this book deals with tourism in Rajasthan and India as tourist destinations and considers why people travel to countries such as India and states such as Rajasthan. It also deals with sociological and anthropological analyses of different kinds of tourists and relates these discussions to tourism in India and to Indian culture. I offer some statistics on tourism in India—statistics, I should point out, whose accuracy must remain somewhat suspect. I also contrast and compare India, which is a hierarchical society, with America, which is an egalitarian one—in theory if not always in practice. And I apply the theories of a social anthropologist, Mary Douglas, and other social scientists, about cultures and lifestyles to India and the choice tourists make to travel there, or anywhere else.

This part of the book deals with research I carried out before coming to India; it focuses on images of India in the popular mind and on typical tours to Rajasthan. It might be described as "Imaginary India," or the India that one finds in books and on the Internet, where there are chat rooms and blogs on India. India currently has an advertising campaign based on the slogan "Incredible !ndia," which I discuss in the second part of the book on "Semiotic Rajasthan," where I offer a brief discussion of semiotic theory and apply it to a number of aspects of life in Rajasthan and India that struck my attention.

The last part of the book deals with "Remembered Rajasthan," and with my experiences as I traveled there. I kept notes on our trip and have used them to write this section of the book. I suggest that travelers generally pass through three stages when it comes to visiting a foreign country: one involves anticipating the trip, the second involves taking the trip, and the third involves remembering the trip. These three stages form the heart of this book.

To prepare for this investigation, I read a number of books about India, from various guidebooks to Jawaharlal Nehru's *The Discovery of India* originally published in 1946. In that book, he discusses the difficulty of trying to understand India:

> India with all her infinite charm and variety began to grow on me more and more, and yet the more I saw of her, the more I realized how very difficult it was for me or for anyone else to grasp the ideas she had embodied. It was not her wide spaces that eluded me, or even her diversity, but some depth of soul which I could not fathom, though I had occasional and tantalizing glimpses of it. (1946/1999: 58-59)

Nehru suggests that India is like an old palimpsest that has layers and layers of thoughts written on it, none of which are completely hidden. These thoughts permeate our unconscious selves, he adds, and they merge together to create the complicated and mysterious personality of India, where there is outward diversity and incredible variety yet, at the same time, a certain "oneness" that holds India together. Trying to fathom what Nehru describes as India's "sphinx-like face" with its "mocking smile" is one of the difficulties anyone writing about India faces.

# Preface

## An Overview of Rajasthan

Rajasthan is the second most popular tourist destination in India, after Kerala. Many tourists who go to India follow what is called "The Golden Triangle." This involves, generally speaking, flying to New Delhi and spending a day or two there. Then tourists move on to Agra for a day or two to see the Taj Mahal—the most iconic of Indian tourist sites. Finally, they visit Jaipur, in Rajasthan. There are numerous tours that tie the Golden Triangle tour to extended visits to other cities in Rajasthan and other parts of India.

Many of the Rajasthan tours describe themselves as "Forts and Palaces" or "Rajasthan Heritage" tours, and visit cities such as Bikaner, Jaisalmer, Jodhpur, and Udaipur. This book focuses on Rajasthan, but also includes the Golden Triangle sites and is based on a long and comprehensive tour my wife and I took in Rajasthan.

According to *The Lonely Planet India* (2005) the Indian state of Rajasthan, which has a larger land area than Italy, has a population of 56 million people, and an area of 342,000 square kilometers (132,000 square miles). Its most important languages are Hindi and Rajasthani. It borders on Pakistan, to the west and on Gujarat to the south, and Punjab and Uttar Pradesh to the north.

The population density in Rajasthan is approximately 165 persons per square kilometer, which is half of the population density of India as a whole. To get some idea of what this density figure means, it is useful to compare the land areas and population densities in Rajasthan with those in several American states.

| Place | Land Area in Square Miles |
| --- | --- |
| Rajasthan | 132,000 |
| California | 165,000 |
| New Mexico | 121,000 |
| Italy | 116,000 |

Source: http:www.mohfw.nic.in/NRHM/State percent20Files/raj.htm

**Figure P.1**
**Typical Huge Fort in Rajasthan**

Thus, Rajasthan, with 132,000 square miles, is smaller than California and larger than New Mexico and Italy. Rajasthan is the second largest state, in terms of land area, in India. When it comes to density of population the following statistics are of interest. These figures for American states come from the United States Census.

| Place | Population Density Per Square Kilometer |
|---|---|
| Rajasthan | 165 persons |
| New Jersey | 438 persons |
| New York | 195 persons |
| Delaware | 157 persons |

Source: http://www.census.gov/popest/states/NST-ann-est.html

We see, then, that Rajasthan has a population density similar to that of Delaware and considerably smaller than those of New Jersey and New York.

I chose to write about Rajasthan because it is impossible to do justice to a country as vast and complex as India but I would hope that my discussions of various aspects of culture and society in Rajasthan would have implications for India and some of my analyses deal with India and Indian culture, in general. It is difficult to separate some aspects of Rajasthani culture from Indian culture. It is always a problem to separate a region from the country in which it is found. I chose Rajasthan because it is more easily managed and because I could visit most of it on our tour. It is difficult to make generalizations about any country, but India is particularly difficult to deal with. So Rajasthan is the figure that I will be investigating against the background of India.

In *Culture Shock India: Survival Guide to Customs and Etiquette,* Gitanjili Koanad writes (2005:5):

> If you lay a map of India over a map of Europe, it covers the area from Denmark to Libya, and from Spain to Russia. As different as these European countries are, so are the different parts of India. More than a billion people live on 3, 287,590 sq. km (1,269,345.6 sq miles) of land. According to the authoritative publication, *People of India*, these billion are members of 4,636 separate communities that belong to at least four distinct racial groups. They speak 325 different languages and practice more than seven religions (sometimes two or more at the same time).

Each of the areas in India has, she adds, a distinct culture so Uttar Pradesh is as different from a state such as Tamil Nadu as Italy is from Finland.

We see, then, that there are many different cultures in India, so my study of Rajasthan can only offer hints of what Indian culture, broadly speaking, is like. We can say the same about all large countries, to varying degrees, where different regions have different cultures or subcultures. Yet, it is possible to offer some suggestions, along the way, about what is "Indian" about India and what is distinctive about Rajasthan.

Why tourists decide to go where they go is something of a mystery to tourism scholars. I will say something about this matter shortly. In some cases, a country, region, or city becomes "hot" or "the place to go," and tourists then flock to those places. People may have seen a city or some of a country in some film and decide to see the place for themselves. A travel book may become popular and that induces people to visit that place described in the book. Some tourists avoid these popular places and visit countries where there are fewer tourists, in search of what they hope will be more "authentic" experiences.

In my case, I suspect that there were a number of factors involved in my choice of India as a place to visit. In 1949 and 1950, when I was a high school student, I went to Saturday art classes at the Museum of Fine Arts in Boston. One of the instructors, Alma LeBrecht, was a world traveler and over lunch often described her adventures in India, China, and other lands. In those days, foreign travel wasn't as easy or inexpensive as it is now, and I never thought I would have the opportunity to visit such countries. So the idea of visiting India may have been percolating in my unconscious for more than fifty years.

There were, no doubt, other factors as well. Some wonderful Indian novels I read may have had a role. Perhaps some superb Indian food that my wife and I enjoyed in a small restaurant in Ho Chi Minh City was another reason. It could have been a flyer I received from a travel agency that listed what seemed to be a very interesting tour in northern India. Maybe it was Satyajit Ray's *Apu* trilogy that I saw many years ago? Whatever the case, in 2006 my wife and I decided that we would take a tour of India in December of that year and I started investigating Indian travel agencies, looking for interesting tours.

I discovered there were a large number of agencies offering tours everywhere in India. There were any number of different tours in Rajasthan, as well, depending upon how much time one wanted to spend there and whether one also wanted to visit other areas of India and other cities. One thing that was a nuisance was that most of the tourism agencies didn't have the prices of their tours on the websites. One reason for this is that the price of a given tour is based on the kind of hotels in which you choose to stay. Some sites gave prices for "Budget hotels, Deluxe hotels, and Luxury hotels." I contacted a number of these agencies and then they sent detailed descriptions of their tours along with prices for various hotel options. Almost all of them were for private tours in a car with a driver and a guide. The hotels all provided breakfasts.

I thought it would be more interesting to find a group tour of some kind and so I chose a company, Jasbhag Tours, which offered a small six-person group tour in a nine-seat bus. The tour had the advantage, also, of providing dinners as well as breakfasts every day. That relieved us of the problem of finding places to eat dinner every day, and suggested, I thought, that I might have the chance to avoid the typical tourist foods and have a more interesting choice of foods. I entered into an e-mail correspondence with an agent named Amandeep Singh, who was extremely patient with me and answered all of my questions in numerous e-mail messages with good humor.

It turned out that the other four people on the tour cancelled their booking so my wife and I and a driver named Roshan, partial to all things Rajasthani, toured Rajasthan in a large Honda automobile.

# Acknowledgments

In recent years I became interested in using what might be described as an ethnographic or ethno-semiotic approach to tourism studies and have written ethno-semiotic analyses of ocean cruising and tourism in Vietnam, Thailand, and Bali. I find these projects enormously interesting and challenging and hope that my analyses and interpretations of important symbols and significant aspects of everyday life in the countries I have written about will be of use not only to scholars and students but to tourists who wish to have a better understanding of their experiences in the countries I have investigated.

Let me also express my gratitude to the people of India whose remarkable warmth and friendliness made my trip there so pleasant.

The statistics in the book come from a variety of sources: newspaper and magazine articles, radio programs, books, and material on the Internet.

I took all of the photographs used in this book.

# Part 1

## Rajasthan as a Tourist Destination—An Analytic Perspective

# 1

# Tourism in India and Rajasthan

*Rajasthan, the Land of the Kings, is India's most colour-charged state. Half desert, half bony hills, the everyday is shot with searing colour—brilliant fabrics flash like flames against the stark landscape. You'll experience these saturated shocks of color everywhere—a sea of turbans clustered under a village tree, rural women in traditional dress, saris drying on parched riverbed.*

*Like a legend come to life, the state is packed with magical towns and cities; sky-blue Jodhpur; Jaipur, painted dusty pink; Jaisamer, a golden sandcastle; Udaipur, shimmering bone-white; and Pushkar, clinging around its holy lake.*
—Sarina Singh et al., *Lonely Planet India*

It is difficult to get reliable statistics on tourism in India and Rajasthan, and other aspects of life there, but I have managed to obtain some statistics that seem credible. They are not all up to date, and we have to take them with a grain of salt—but they seem reasonable and based on figures I obtained from a number of different sources, they don't seem to be inflated (http:www/indiainvites.com/dataindia2003.htm).

India is a large country, approximately 1,270,000 square miles. It has a population of more than one billion people—one which, it has been estimated, will reach 1.5 billion people in another ten or twenty years. To put things in perspective, the United States is 3,615,000 square miles—almost three times as large as India, yet the population of the United States is approximately 300 million people. There are less than a third as many people in the United States as India, which gives an idea of how crowded India is.

## Foreign Tourism in India

The figures below, taken from the Ministry of Tourism, show that foreign tourism in India has grown considerably in just a few years.

| Year | Foreign Tourist Arrivals |
|---|---|
| 2004 | 3,457,477 |
| 2005 | 3,718,680 |
| 2006 | 4,429,915 |

Source: http://www.fhrai.com/mag-news/magTourismStatisticsIndia.asp

To put these figures in perspective, let me offer statistics on tourism in European countries and in Vietnam and Thailand for 2005.

If India had only 3.7 million foreign tourists in 2005, we can see that there are a relatively small number of international tourists who visit the country. Thailand, with only 65 million people, has almost three times as many foreign tourists as India. But, as the figures show, foreign tourism in India has been increasing at a rapid rate in recent years.

Where do foreign tourists to India come from? That information was provided by a site on the Internet dealing with tourist statistics for 2004. I will offer statistics on tourist arrivals from the top eight countries. All of these tables are my compilations (source: http://www.pibbng.kar.nic.in/23_11_05_10.pdf).

I have rounded off the number of arrivals to the nearest thousand. Other statistics I've found on the Internet show that Australia, Singapore, the Netherlands, Italy, Nepal, Israel and South Korea also send relatively large numbers of tourists to India. Sri Lanka, Malaysia, Nepal, and South Korea

Table 1.1
Tourism Statistics in European Countries, Vietnam, and Thailand, 2005

| Country | Number of Visitors | Population |
|---|---|---|
| France | 76.0 million | 58 million |
| Spain | 55.5 million | 40 million |
| United States | 45.5 million | 300 million |
| Italy | 36.5 million | 57 million |
| United Kingdom | 29.9 million | 58 million |
| Mexico | 19.8 million | 100 million |
| Austria | 19.9 million | 8 million |
| Thailand | 12 million | 65 million |
| Vietnam | 3.43 million | 83 million |

Source: http://www.unwto.org/fact/eng/pdf/indicators/1TA_Europe.pdf

## Table 1.2
## Country of Origin of Foreign Tourists in India for 2004

| Country | Number of Arrivals | Percentage |
|---|---|---|
| USA | 520,000 | 15.5 |
| UK | 499,000 | 14.8 |
| Sri Lanka | 129,000 | 3.8 |
| France | 133,000 | 4.0 |
| Canada | 134,000 | 4.0 |
| Germany | 102,000 | 3.0 |
| Japan | 98,000 | 2.9 |
| Malaysia | 83,000 | 2.5 |

are relatively close to India, but the rest of the countries are quite distant, especially the United States. It takes more than twenty hours of flying time from San Francisco to get to India, using Hong Kong as a staging point.

One Internet site, Neoncarrot, devoted to statistics about India (www.neoncarrot.co.uk/h_aboutIndia_tourism_stats.html), reports that approximately 300,000 Britons visit India each year and states that about 60 percent of foreign visitors go to the northern states. It also says that there are 300 million domestic tourists in India in a typical year—a figure that represents about 30 percent of the population and a figure which Neoncarrot suggests includes weekend trips, pilgrimages and that kind of thing.

Neoncarrot gives a figure of more than three million visitors to the Taj Mahal in 2003, which would suggest that an extremely high percentage of visitors to India go to the Taj Mahal, India's most visited tourist attraction. If three million foreign tourists visit the Taj Mahal in a typical year, that suggests that on any given day there are around 8,000 tourists there.

It seems, then, that a large percentage of foreign visitors to India make it a point to go to Agra to see the Taj Mahal, India's most iconic tourist site. How many of them take a "Golden Triangle Tour" from New Delhi and also visit Jaipur in Rajasthan is hard to say, but it is reasonable to suggest that a considerable number of them do so. The foreign tourism figures are complicated by the fact that many of the foreign arrivals may be Indians with American citizenship or Indians currently living in America returning to the country for vacations, family matters, or on business. It is not surprising that tourists from the U.K., U.S. Japan, France, and Germany are among the leaders in foreign tourists in India because these countries are the leading tourism nations in terms of per capital expenses for tourism, in general.

6  The Golden Triangle

**Figure 1.1
A Vegetable Market in Udaipur**

According to the World Tourist Organization, the United Kingdom, Germany, France, Japan, and the United States rank in the order listed in terms of amount of money spent on tourism, so it is reasonable to expect to find tourists from these countries in many different lands, including India (http://www.world-tourism.org/facts/eng.pdf.indicators/top percent20spenders.pdf).

What is so surprising is that the tourism industry in India is so undeveloped, relatively speaking. Let me suggest some reasons why so few foreign tourists, relatively speaking, visit India, even though, as I read on the Internet, many tourists who had gone there said it was a marvelous and in some cases a "life-changing" experience.

Table 1.3
Tourism Expenditures by Countries

| Country | UK | Germany | France | Japan | USA |
|---|---|---|---|---|---|
| Expenditure | 56.57 Billion | 71 Billion | 28.6 Billion | 38.2 Billion | 65.6 Billion |
| Population | 60 Million | 82 Million | 60 Million | 120 Million | 300 Million |
| Per Capita | $637 | $575 | $293 | $258 | $222 |
| Ranking | 1 | 2 | 3 | 4 | 5 |

## A Brief Summary of Statistics on India, Rajasthan, and Tourism in India

What follows is a statistical portrait of India and Rajasthan, and the tourism industry there. These figures will enable us to get some perspective on Indian society and culture and the role that tourism is playing there and globally. It brings together some data that has been offered previously and adds some new material. My statistics come from the following sources:

> www.incredibleindia.com; www.rajasthantourism.gov.in; the World Tourism Organization; www.rajasthan.gov.in; and www.neoncarrot.co.uk/h; and UNWTOWorld Tourism Barometer.

**World Tourism Statistics**
735 billion dollars spent by tourists in 2006
806 (approximately) million international travelers in 2005
Every ninth person in the world works in travel and tourism industry
1.6 billion world travellers in 2010 (estimated)

**India: A Statistical Portrait**
1,270,000 Square Miles (USA: 3,600,000 Square Miles)
1.1 billion people
50 percent of Indians are under 25
680,000 villages
4635 identifiable communities
400 million cattle and buffalos (one sixth of world's cows and one half of
    world's buffalos)
60 percent of milk in India comes from buffalos
Cow dung is the most important fuel source in India
50 percent of rural Indians have electric lights
Cell phone use: 100 million in 2005 (3 million in 2000)
4 percent of people in India have refrigerators

260 persons per square kilometer population density
40 percent of Indians live on one dollar (or less) per day
Average salary less than $1000 a year
Less than 50 percent have electricity
50,000 Indians with income over $225,000 per year
300,000,000 estimated middle class Indians
300,000,000 living in poverty
35 million taxpayers
10 percent of Indians have "formal" jobs
1 million engineering graduates per year
Growth in economy of more than 8 percent in recent years
Television channels 150 in 2005 (1 in 19991)
Four races
325 languages
25 scripts
Seven major religions
3.37 million foreign tourist arrivals in 2005
367 million domestic tourists in 2004
4.8 billion US dollars earned from tourism in 2004
Ranks 44 in world's top 60 tourism destinations
60 percent of foreign tourists visit the "Golden Triangle" of Delhi, Agra and Jaipur
144 million Indians work in travel and tourism industry

> *Note*: Some of the statistics offered above were found in a review by William Grimes (in the January 17, 2007, page B9 edition of *The New York Times*) of Edward Luce's *In Spite of the Gods: The Strange Rise of Modern India*. Other data comes from K. N. Panikkar's essay "Outsider as Enemy: Politics of Rewriting History in India" found on Google Scholar and other statistics come from various sources such as newspaper articles and information on the Internet and websites mentioned above.

**Rajasthan: A Statistical Portrait**
Total area: 342,000 square kilometers (132,000 square miles)
Thar Desert: 213,000 square kilometers (82,000 square miles)
10 percent of India's geographical area
56,000,000 people (80 million estimated by 2016)
61 percent literacy rate
22 percent urban
165 people per square kilometer population density
33 Billion U.S. Dollars Gross State Domestic Product
600,000 foreign tourists visit Rajasthan (or 1.2 million by other estimates)
8000 Rupees per day spent by foreign tourists (around $180.00)
4000 Rupees per day spent by native tourists (around $90.00)
2.5 days (or fourteen days?) on average spent by foreign tourists in Rajasthan
39 heritage hotels in Rajasthan
70 percent of camels in India are in Rajasthan

This figure of 2.5 days spent by foreign tourists strikes me as quite suspect, since tourists doing the Golden Triangle of Delhi, Agra, and Jaipur would be limited to two days in Jaipur and not be able to go anyplace else in Rajasthan.

In addition, some people in the tourism industry who I consulted said most people spend around two weeks touring Rajasthan. This sounds reasonable for aside from Indians from neighboring states, such as Gujarat, foreign tourists generally have to fly for rather long periods to get to India and it is reasonable to assume they stay there for several weeks or more.

> *Note*: In an article "A Passage to India's Future" from the Feb. 4-5, 2006 edition of the *Wall Street Journal,* Stan Sesser writes "some 1.2 million people visited Rajasthan last year—triple the number that came just three years ago" (p.4). He does not say with these visitors were all foreign tourists or whether some of them were from India. He also writes "The U.S. has now displaced Britain as the No. 1 source of visitors to India—some 600,000 Americans traveled there last year."

In his book, *Tristes Tropiques,* the eminent anthropologist Claude Lévi-Strauss laments the changes that, he suggests, had taken place in the world as they relate to travel and tourism:

> I should have liked to live in the age of *real* travel, when the spectacle on offer had not yet been blemished, contaminated, and confounded; then I could have seen Lahore not as I saw it, but as it appeared to "Bernier, Tavernier, Manucci.... There's no end, of course, to such conjectures. When was the right moment to see India? At what period would the study of the Brazilian savage have yielded the purest satisfaction and the savage himself have been at his peak?... The alternative is inescapable: either I am a traveller in ancient times, and faced with a prodigious spectacle which would be almost entirely unintelligible to me and might, indeed, provoke me to mockery or disgust; or I am a traveller of our own day, hastening in search of a vanished reality. (44,45).

What the statistics I have just offered suggest is that Lévi-Strauss was too pessimistic about the age of "real" travel being over. He wondered what the right time to see India had been. But for an ever-increasing number of people from all over the world, the right time to see India seems to be now and the forces of modernization and homogenization that he feared would lead to a boring monoculture are far removed from the India foreign visitors experience—especially in states such as Rajasthan and in countless villages and other parts of India where a culture that is remarkably foreign to Westerners is to be found. We can see this when we examine the image of India on the Internet.

## The Image of India in Frommer's Website: Travel Talk India

We must remember that there is often a considerable difference between the image people have of a country and what that country is really like. An image, for our purposes, is a commonly held picture of a country, a widely accepted set of beliefs about what a foreign country is like, and what tourists in that country can expect. Images are similar in nature to stereotypes, except that stereotypes tend to be negative and focus on specific groups of people (ethnic, racial, and religious) and images are more general.

We can get an insight into what potential tourists to India worry about by looking at Frommer's Travel Talk website devoted to India. Let me list the first ten or so discussion topics on the site for March 31, 2006. I have made minor grammatical and spelling changes here and there to this list and the other material that follows because writers of these messages aren't always careful about what they write:

**Poverty, Beggars & Filth in India** (37 messages)
Go to India NOW! Used Indian Moments (12 messages)
Trip to Taj Mahal (4 messages)
Traveling to India Summer 2006...(2 messages)
When to go (2 messages)
Dining in India—How risky? (2 messages)
Orchha (Jhansi) to Jaipur (1 message)
Trip Report: 30 Days in India and Bhutan (new)
OAT Tour to India/Bhutan (2 messages)
What to do in Bangalore in 1-2 days (1 message)
3 Weeks in India—Advice Please (1 message)

From this list we can see some of the topics that are of concern to people planning to visit India. Let me cite, here, some of what was written on the query about "poverty, beggars and filth" in India.

*Poverty, Beggars and Filth in India*

I hate to bring up such a sensitive topic but clearly it's one that would apply to India.

> I had wholeheartedly began planning a 2 week luxury trip to Northern India...having read the many posts here and having seen of the good looking hotels/palaces that can be stayed at along the way. But then I saw a film that showed the extensive poverty, begging and disgusting filth found around. In particular, it showed bodies floating in the Ganges near Varnesi, etc. This made me question whether I would be nuts to even subject myself and my wife to this.

The author of this post points out that he and his wife have traveled in such countries as Egypt, Morocco, and Turkey, which are also very poor. He wonders whether going to India would be "too extreme" a trip to undertake.

This posting offers an insight into the anxieties many people feel about going to India. Tourists considering visiting India wonder whether they will be subjecting themselves to experiences that will be too "extreme" and too intense for them—experiences which will cause so much culture shock and emotionally exhaust them to the point that their trip will be unpleasant or worse.

There were thirty-seven replies to this query when I visited it in April of 2006, most of which encouraged the person who posted the query to go to India. Many of them said that a trip to India was a life-changing experience. As one of the responders, a backpacker, wrote, India assaults the senses of visitors, but it is a magnificent country and all visitors leave as changed persons. Another person who posted a message was more negative and wrote about feeling helpless in India and said the trip was great but the feeling of helplessness was very frustrating.

Another posting on the Frommer India site asks about dining in India. Many potential tourists are afraid of contracting a terrible disease while in India from the food and ask about ways of protecting themselves. Writers offer various suggestions about how to avoid getting sick from the food, such as not eating anything that hasn't been cooked, just eating vegetarian food and making sure that you open every water bottle you purchase at a restaurant.

There is also the matter of the hotels in India. There are some world-class hotels in many cities that are very expensive and are equal or superior to many hotels in America or Europe. And there are backpacker hotels that are very inexpensive, but not suitable for the average middle-aged, middle-class tourist. It is the three-star hotels that are the problem. If you look at the images of these hotels on their websites, they look very good. And yet, if you read the comments of some visitors (which I found on the TripAdvisor website) you find that some of the rooms in these three star hotels are dingy, sometimes the hot water doesn't run very well, and that the staffs of some hotels are surly and unpleasant. We found no dingy rooms during our visit and some of the hotels we stayed at were quite wonderful.

## TripAdvisor Postings on Indian Hotels

TripAdvisor is an Internet travel site that, among other things, posts reviews that people write about hotels they have visited. In some cases, you find almost unanimous agreement from travelers who post comments about the hotels they've stayed at on TripAdvisor, but in others you find one person who hated everything about a hotel and another person who found it magical and enchanting. It is reasonable to assume, then, that people who write evaluations to sites such as TripAdvisor are strongly motivated one way or another and all reviews must be taken with a grain of salt.

Let me offer an example of the kind of conflicting reviews one can find on this site. These reviews were taken from the TripAdvisor site listing hotels in major Rajasthan cities. I chose two reviews of the Trident Hilton hotel in Udaipur.

*Poor Food and Service*

My wife and I were most disappointed with our 3 days in this hotel.

The Buffet was very limited and the food was cold. It was the worst experience we had in our 4 weeks in India. Also the so-called Gymnasium was a joke. (Hotel stay took place during March 2006)

*Best Hotel in Rajasthan*

This was the first hotel where we were treated respectfully. Okay, it sometimes was a little overboard, but it was still appreciated…This was also the first hotel we had seen 1) room service menus and 2) directory of services. After staying in so-called 5 star hotels, this was a breath of fresh air. (November 2005)

These two comments represent extremes, with many other people posting reviews that were positive in some respects and negative in others.

Reading the postings on various TripAdvisor sites, on the Lonely Planet "Thorn Tree" site, and on Frommer's "Travel Talk" on India provides a person with a wide range of commentaries on all kinds of topics related to India, from finding good hotels in Delhi to taking tours, places to visit, and optimal times to go to India. Some of the people who write on the Frommer site are Indians who are trying to be helpful and others are people who have been to India and have suggestions to make. There are also a large number of comments on India on numerous travel blogs that can be consulted

## A Summary of Anxieties Felt by Tourists Planning a Trip to India

Let me summarize some of the anxieties that tourists planning a trip to India feel. Whether all of these anxieties are based on fact is not the point; if people *think* they will experience something in India, their thoughts will affect their decision-making. This list comes from reading the Frommer's "Travel Talk" postings and from other sources:

**Figure 1.2
A Haveli with Decorations in Mandawa**

India has terrible poverty which becomes depressing to tourists.
India is filthy. People defecate on the streets and cow dung is everywhere.
India is full of beggars who pester tourists mercilessly.
Indian food poses a health risk due to the water and poorly cooked food.
India is too crowded, being "wall-to-wall" with people.
India is terribly polluted.
Indian hotels are not satisfactory. Many have dingy rooms and surly staff.
India lacks the proper infrastructure for tourism.
Indian bureaucracies are infuriating.

This list suggests that there are formidable obstacles that present themselves to travelers contemplating touring in India. The question

14    The Golden Triangle

**Figure 1.3**
**A Thali Meal Served at the Hotel Karni Bhavan Palace in Bikaner**

then arises—why do people go to India in spite of these obstacles. To understand why foreign tourists visit India, and Rajasthan, in the next chapter I will describe some typical tours that are available there, and then I will discuss a number of the gratifications that travel in India offers to visitors. I will also discuss different kinds of tourists and will say something about the kinds of tourists who are attracted to India. India may pose formidable problems for tourists, but those who go there do so because they think the rewards will be great.

The first page of the *Let's Go India & Nepal* guidebook (2003) explains the rewards that a trip to India offers in graphic terms:

> With a population that has just topped one billion, India bursts at the seams with dozens of different cultures and a vibrant variety to mach the magnitude of its sheer numbers. Birthplace of three of the world's oldest religions—Hinduism, Buddhism, and Jainism—India today accommodates countless others and struggles to maintain its secular facade as the world's largest democracy. .. From the moment you step down from the plane, your senses will be under assault. The sublime beauty of India's natural scenery and towering temples are as likely to overwhelm as the ubiquitous smells of dirt, dust, and dung. (1).

The author of this material offers a description of the assault on the senses that occurs when one visits India, and adds that while many tourists

**Figure 1.4**
**The Oberoi Udaivilas Hotel in Lake Pichola, Udaipur**

can't wait to get out of India to a "safer" place, others fall in love with it and stay in India because of their passionate love of the country.

I recently had a chat with a neighbor of mine who had just come back from her second trip to India. She said that she and her husband were planning to return for a third trip shortly.

"I guess you like India," I said to her.

She smiled. "It's not only that I like India," she replied. "I'm absolutely *obsessed* with India."

What India promises, then, is an experience beyond the dimensions of tourism in most countries—a visit that truly is "incredible" and, for some people, life changing. A popular backpacker sentiment I found somewhere expresses the impact that India has on many visitors and is very revealing. "When you're in India, you spend a lot of time figuring out how escape from it, but when you're out of India, you spend a lot of timing figuring how to get back in."

# 2

# Tours and Tourists in Rajasthan

*Opler has applied a themal analysis to the culture of North India in which he distinguishes the following themes:*
1. *Divisiveness (Family cleavages, subcast divisions and factions)*
2. *Hierarchy (The grading of castes, of supernaturals, and of parts of the body.)*
3. *Concern for right action or dharma*
4. *Concern for ritual purity and fear of pollution. (Untouchability, attitudes toward leather and other polluting substances, ideas about menstruation, food taboos, frequent bathing for ritual purification.) . . .*
5. *Ascendancy of the male principle, with some fear and suspicion of the female principle.) . . .*
6. *Familism. (The family takes precedence over the individual . . . )*
7. *Balance, consensus, or harmony . . .*
8. *Nonviolence (Vegetarianism. Fasting as a form of protest.)*
9. *High value of intellect, rationalism.*
10. *Transcendentalism. (Other worldly emphasis . . . )*
11. *Conception of rhythm of existence. (Beliefs in cycles of time. Fatalism.)*
    *Oppler points out that some of these themes (such as Male ascendancy and Hierarchy) support each other, while some are at odds with each other . . .*
    —Victor Barnouw, *Culture and Personality*

By searching "Rajasthan Tours" on Google, I found numerous companies in India that provided tours of Rajasthan, as well as other areas in India. Many of these tours in Rajasthan go to the same important cities; they differ slightly from one to another in terms of how much time one wishes to spend in Rajasthan and what kind of hotels one wishes to stay at: budget (one star), so-called deluxe (three star), or luxury (five star) hotels. There are also super-deluxe hotels that have been awarded six stars. The Indian travel agencies all have basic tours but will design their tours according to the wishes of each tourist and thus can provide one-week, fourteen-day, eighteen-day, or longer tours of Rajasthan. The tours have titles such as "Golden Triangle and Culture of Rajasthan," "Heritage Rajasthan," and "Forts and Palaces of Rajasthan." There are also tours that visit Rajasthan and then venture out of the state to places like Mumbai and southern India. There are also "North to South" tours in India and countless other variations. You can modify any of the tours that are available or arrange for any kind of tour you want.

I found that when I sent an e-mail inquiry to tourist companies in India, I received a detailed itinerary and information about the tours, hotel choices, and prices almost immediately. One travel agent even called me from India.

## Two Typical Rajasthan Itineraries

Below I offer two typical itineraries in Rajasthan, including the tour I chose, the Jasbhag "Tempo" Tour (24 days, 23 nights). The other tour was a heritage "Indian Forts and Palaces Tour" (19 days, 18 nights) offered by a different company. You can see from the number of hours it takes to go from one place to another that there is a great deal of driving involved in these tours, even though the distances in terms of kilometers might not be that great.

The Jasbhag tour involved around forty-seven hours of driving from city to city as well as other hours involved in sightseeing at various destinations. The Heritage tour involved around fifty-three hours of travel between cities as well as other hours involved in sightseeing. It is obvious that traveling in Rajusthan, even in air conditioned cars and other vehicles, is very demanding and time consuming. And traveling to India from the United States takes a very long time, so India is not a very easy place to visit. But tourists who go there, especially from the Western world, have to assume it is worth the expense and the physical strains involved in going there and traveling around. There are other kinds of tours in which tourists fly from place to place, but that means they only see bits and pieces of India—though that kind of experience is valuable in itself and of use to people who do not have the stamina or physical ability to visit India other ways.

## The Gratifications of Tourism in Rajasthan

What follows is an adaptation of work done by media sociologists and psychologists on the uses and gratifications provided to audiences by different kinds of media texts. Instead of investigating possible effects of exposure to media, a number of social scientists studied what gratifications various kinds of radio programs, television shows, and books provided to people and the way they "used" them to deal with problems they faced or find "escape" from their daily routines. We can do the same thing for tourism, which provides numerous gratifications to people. I have already alluded to this matter in a general way in my quotation from the *Let's Go India & Nepal* guidebook. Here are some more specific considerations.

## Table 2.1
### a. Typical Forts and Palaces Tours in Rajasthan

| JASBHAG TOUR | HERITAGE TOUR |
|---|---|
| 1. Arrive Delhi | Arrive Delhi |
| 2. Delhi to Jaipur (5 hours) | Delhi Sightseeing |
| 3. Jaipur Tour | Delhi to Mandawa (6 hours) |
| 4. Jaipur Excursion | Mandawa to Bikaner (4 hours) |
| 5. Jaipur to Mandawa (3 hours) | Bikaner to Khimsar (3 hours) |
| 6. Mandawa to Bikaner (4 hours) | Kimsar to Jaisalmer (7 hours) |
| 7. Bikaner Excursion to Deshinok | Jaisalmer Tour, Camel Ride |
| 8. Bikaner to Jaisalmer (6 hours) | Jaisalmer to Jodhpur (6 hours) |
| 9. Jaisalmer Camel Safari | Jodhpur to Luni (1 hour) |
| 10. Jaisalmer | Luni to Ranakpur (4 hours) |
| 11. Jaisalmer to Jodhpur (5.5 hours) | Ranakpur to Udaipur (2 hours) |
| 12. Jodhpur | Udaipur to Deogarh (4 hours) |
| 13. Jodhpur to Mt. Abu (6 hours) | Deogarh to Samode (6 hours) |
| 14. Mt. Abu Tour | Samode to Jaipur (1 hour) |
| 15. Mt. Abu to Udaipur (4 hours) | Jaipur Tour |
| 16. Udaipur Boat Ride | Jaipur to Agra (5 hours) |
| 17. Udaipur Excursion to Ranakpur | Agra to Delhi (4 hours) |
| 18. Udaipur Excursion to Chittaurgarh | Delhi to return flight |
| 19. Udairpur to Sawai Madhopur | |
| 20. Sawai Madhopur | |
| 21. Sawai Madhopur to Agra (6 hours) | |
| 22. Agra Taj Mahal Tour | |
| 23. Agra to Delhi (4 hours) | |
| 24. Delhi to Return flight | |

### b. Distances between cities on Jasbhag Tour

| City | Kilometers | Hours for Trip |
|---|---|---|
| Delhi to Jaipur | 265 | 5 |
| Jaipur to Mandawa | 180 | 3 |
| Mandawa to Bikaner | 200 | 3 |
| Bikaner to Jaisalmer | 325 | 6 |
| Jaisalmer to Jodphur | 300 | 5.5 |
| Jodphur to Mt. Abu | 300 | 5.5 |
| Mt. Abu to Udaipur | 200 | 4 |
| Udaipur to Sawadi Madhopur | 300 | 5.5 |
| Sawadi Madhopur to Agra | 300 | 5.5 |
| Agra to Delhi | 200 | 4 |
| **TOTAL** | **2700** | **47** |

## *India is Exotic*

Whatever else one might wish to say about Rajasthan and India, its culture and daily life is seen as exotic and far different from the experiences one has in the United States or Europe. Many tourists seek the exotic as a counter to their everyday life experiences and thus India's exotic nature is a powerful draw for them. The campaign of the Indian tourism industry, "Incredible !ndia," plays into this matter of a desire for the exotic in many tourists—a desire to do something different from visiting France or Italy or other countries which aren't that much different from one's own country.

Let me offer a chart that shows the difference between the exotic and what I suggest is its opposite, the everyday. This chart is adapted from my book *Deconstructing Travel: Cultural Perspectives on Tourism* and offers what might be describe as extreme differences or what the sociologist Max Weber (who wrote a great deal on India) would describe as "ideal types" that do not always exist in the real world.

| The Exotic | The Everyday |
| --- | --- |
| Distant | Near |
| The past | The present |
| Strange | Familiar |
| Ancient, traditional | Modern |
| The hut | The skyscraper |
| The bazaar | The supermarket |
| Hindu temples | Catholic Cathedrals |
| Ethnic cuisine | Euro-American cuisine |
| Mechanical | Electronic |
| Turbans, robes | Suits |

Since tourists generally are in search of that which is different, what is exotic to an urban person from western Europe or the United States about India is part of the everyday for Indians, especially those who are from rural areas. They, in turn, would find the urban everyday life in Europe or the United States "exotic," since it is so different from their lives. Whether these polarities have as much meaning as they once did, in a media age and global village is now open to question.

*Curiosity about India Can be Satisfied*

Many tourists travel to satisfy their curiosity about some country that has attracted their attention. For many people, India represents a curious combination of a country with modern high technology in some sections of the country and with ancient lifestyles in others. Our curiosity about what Indian life and culture is really like—beyond what we read in newspapers and magazines—extends to Indian arts, cuisine, and various aspects of everyday life in India.

*Experiencing Extreme Emotions in a Controlled Situation*

Rajasthan (and India in general) promises tourists "extreme" experiences—which is very alluring to certain kinds of tourists in search of adventure and an escape from the routines of first world tourism. The poverty and other seemingly "negative" aspects of India function, then, as an attraction to many people who are in search of powerful and even life-changing experiences. This is one of the things that tourism in India promises. As many people who posted messages on the Frommer's website explained, "after India you'll never be the same." The implications of these statements are that a trip in India confronts tourists with dimensions of experience that were beyond anything they had ever known and that this was enriching and spiritually rewarding, despite the difficulties involved in travelling there.

*Getting in Touch with the Beautiful*

It is the legendary beauty of the Taj Mahal that makes it the most important tourist attraction in India and one of the most iconic tourism sites in the world. The "proper" way to experience the Taj Mahal, tourist guides explain, is at dawn, which enhances the experience. Seeing the sun rise over the Taj Mahal is a "world class" tourist experience—on a par with visiting the Great Wall of China or the Egyptian Pyramids. In addition to the Taj Mahal, there are numerous wonderful and interesting forts and castles and other buildings and beautiful natural sites in India that are appealing to tourists, many of whom are in search of beauty which they feel enriches their lives.

*Experiencing the Ugly*

This gratification is the polar opposite of the desire to experience the beautiful and is tied to it. For if there is something that is beautiful, there must be something that is ugly, since, as Saussure pointed out in his *Course in General Linguistics* (1966:20), "in language there are only differences" and concepts take their meaning differentially. This suggests that the extremes of beauty which many tourists seek require extremes of ugly to be meaningful, and thus the crushing weight of wall-to-wall humanity in the cities makes the serenity and emptiness in the Thar desert in Rajasthan all the more meaningful.

*Experiencing Extreme Empathy*

However tourists react to what they consider to be the "ugly" aspects of Indian life—the beggars, the cows wandering around, the people defecating on the streets, the squalor—travel in India seems to have the effect, with most tourists, of enhancing their empathy with the people of India. The friendliness and hospitality of Indian people is legendary and many tourists have commented on wonderful experiences they've had with people in India. Thus many tourists find that their experiences in India give them a new respect for all people and an appreciation of the incredible difficulties many of them face as they struggle, heroically in some cases, to survive.

\* \* \*

We can see from this list of gratifications that India offers tourists the promise of many powerful experiences, which helps explain why foreign tourists go there. If the roads in India pose problems, because they are so small and so crowded with people and cows, the Indian tourism industry provides "solutions" to these problems by making private tours in air conditioned vehicles with guides inexpensive, if one wishes to stay in budget hotels, and relatively inexpensive for stays in three-star hotels. Still, as my comparison of tours in Rajasthan shows, there is a great deal of driving involved in visiting Rajasthan and, by implication, any other state in India. I should add that India is working hard on its infrastructure and is building many new highways to accommodate tourists and industry.

It takes a special kind of person to undertake tours in India, unless one flies around the country from city to city, as some people do. Tourism scholars have offered a number of different typologies that deal with kinds of tourists. Let me discuss two of the most important: those by Erik Cohen and Stanley Plog.

## Types of Tourists

An Israeli sociologist, Erik Cohen, has done a great deal of work on tourism and has written a number of pioneering books about tourism in Thailand. In a widely quoted article titled "Towards a Sociology of International Tourism" (*Social Research,* 39, No. 1 [1972], pp. 164-183) Cohen offers a typology which suggests there are four different kinds of tourists. Tourism professionals tend to divide tourists into two groups: people on group inclusive tours (GIT) and independent travelers (IT). Cohen describes group tourists in his article as follows:

> The organized mass tourist is the least adventurous and remains largely confined to his "environmental bubble" throughout the trip. The guided tour, conducted in an air conditioned bus, traveling at high speed through a streaming countryside, represents the prototype of the organized mass tourist. This tourist type buys a package tour as if it were just another commodity in the modern mass market. The itinerary for his trip is fixed in advance, and all his stops are well-prepared and guided: he makes almost no decisions for himself and stays almost exclusively in the microenvironment of his home country. Familiarity is at a maximum, novelty at a minimum. (Quoted in Berger, 2004:60)

He offers a list of four kinds of tourists, which I describe briefly:

- *Organized Mass Tourists*
They take what travel professionals describe as Group Inclusive Tours and have little influence on what a tour does. They travel in tour buses, stay in expensive, usually five star, hotels and have very few interactions with the people in the places they are touring, other than at markets, restaurants, and at other buying opportunities their tours provide.

- *Individual Mass Tourists*
They have more control over their time and their itineraries, and may rent cars and drive where they want. They also tend to stay in protective bubbles but interact with natives more than organized mass tourists. Before the development of the Internet they would have booked their tours using a travel agency. In an Internet age, they may take care of all of their arrangements online.

- *Explorers*
Explorers are classified as individual travelers and not as group inclusive tourists. They don't live in the protective bubbles that organized mass tourists and individual mass tourists do. They make all of their arrangements and are interested in interacting as much as possible with people in the countries they visit.

- *Drifters*
They tend to be young backpackers who take the cheapest transportation they can get and who stay in youth hostels or very cheap hotels. It costs a considerable amount of money to fly to India from the United States, but once there drifters can live for very little money since food and housing in India can be very inexpensive if one stays at the cheapest rooms and hotels and avoids expensive restaurants.

Cohen takes a sociological approach, looking for socially based categories of tourists. A different typology comes from Stanley Plog, whose 1984 article "Why Destinations Rise and Fall in Popularity" (*Cornell Hotel and Restaurant Administration Quarterly,* 14, no. 4, pp. 55-59) is one of the most widely cited articles on tourism by tourism scholars. Plog's perspective is based on psychological factors—namely based on attitudes toward risk and adventurousness. There are two polarities: adventurous "allocentrics" and risk-averse, non-adventurous "pyschocentrics."

Plog argues that new destinations are discovered by "allocentrics," who are what Cohen would describe as backpackers and explorers. As these destinations become more and more popular, less adventurous mid-centric tourists start going to them and as they become more developed, with a better tourism infrastructure, better hotels, and more creature comforts, full blown, risk-averse "psychocentrics" start going to them in large numbers. Meanwhile, "allocentrics" have moved on to other destinations, since they don't like being in places full of "psychocentrics."

**Figure 2.1**
**Indian Dancer Balancing Bowls on Her Head**

Thus there is, Plog argues, a cycle that explains why various tourist sites become popular—whether it is cities, regions of countries, or countries and a continuum based on the two polarities:

    P_____NP_____ MC_____NA_____A
**Psychocentric** /Near Psychocentric/ Mid Centric/ Near Allocentric/ **Allocentric**

Plog offers a bell-shaped curved, with relatively small numbers of tourists at either end and large numbers of mid-centric tourists occupying most of the bell.

In recent years, since these articles were written, tourism scholars have offered many other theories about tourism. The development of the Internet has also had a profound influence on the travel industry—revolutionizing it in many ways. Because of the strenuous nature of travel

**Figure 2.2
Rats in the Karni Mata Temple in Deshnok**

in India, it would seem that (using Cohen's typology) there would be relatively few individual mass tourists and mostly organized mass tourists, in tours with varying degrees of separation from the masses of people in India, and some explorers and drifters/backpackers. There are "adventure" travel companies such as Intrepid and Djoser that seem well-suited for explorer types. Interestingly, their tours are often as expensive—if not more expensive—than tours booked with Indian travel agencies that provide air conditioned cars, hotels at various price ranges, and guides. At the top end, there are world-class hotels such as those in the Oberoi chain that charge more than five hundred dollars per night. At the low end, there are hotels that can be had for less than ten dollars per night. So there are many options to the traveler planning a trip to India.

When it comes to applying Plog's typology to India, the statistics on tourism in India suggest that it is at the "near Allocentric" or full "Allocentric" end of the continuum. In his article Plog suggested that Africa and the South Pacific were "Allocentric" places to travel, but he wrote his article in 1984, more than twenty years ago, and tourism has changed considerably since then.

The rapid growth of tourism in India leads me to think that India now is probably a "near Allocentric" destination that is striving to become, and may soon become, a "mid-Allocentric" one. What India promises, as the quotation that begins this chapter suggests, is a culture that is profoundly different from American culture. That is part of India's allure and part of what makes it so fascinating for Americans.

**Figure 2.3
Street Scene in Udaipur**

# 3

# Hierarchical India and Egalitarian America

> *Caste is a European term (from the Spanish or Portuguese casta) and is a bad one to use for India. The confusion is all the greater as caste has been used to translate the two very different concepts of varna and jati. There are four varnas, which in descending hierarchical order, are the brahmins (traditionally priests and teachers), the rajputs or kshatriyas (warriors and rulers), the vaishya (merchants), and the sudra (peasants and common people). Over the centuries, a fifth group, consisting of people engaged in occupations considered to be defiling (such as scavenging or the killing and processing of animals), developed below the four varnas, in a position so lowly as to be regarded as social pariahs. These were known as the untouchables (as contact with them defiled any higher caste Hindu) . . . In terms of day-to-day life, the jati rather than the varna is the significant social group. Except for the Brahmins (who technically regard themselves as a single jati, but in fact are divided into many sub-jati), each of the varnas is internally divided into hundreds of jati (or "castes" in the restricted sense) and many of these jati are in turn divided into sub-jati. Altogether there are many thousands of jati and sub-jati in India. The jati generally has a ruling council, or panchayat. The jati is a solidary social group from which one may be expelled ("outcasting") for severe offenses, but to which one normally belongs by birth and for life.*
> —Pierre L. van den Berghe, *Man in Society: A Biosocial View*

American society is egalitarian in philosophy (though not always in practice) and Indian society is hierarchical in nature (though perhaps not always in practice), with castes and sub-castes of all kinds that shape the lives, to varying degrees, of people in India. As such, the two countries can be described, without stretching credulity too much, as being polar opposites.

## Emerson on American Culture

The great American author Ralph Waldo Emerson described America, in one of his poems, "America, My Country" (1833) as a "land without history." His poem reads as follows (Berger, *Signs in Contemporary Culture,* 2nd edition [1999:161]):

> **America, My Country**
> Land without history, land lying all
> In the plain daylight of the temperate zone.
> 		Thy plain acts
> Without exaggeration done in day;
> Thy interests contested by their manifold good sense.
> In their own clothes without the ornament
> Of bannered army harnessed in uniform.
> Land where—and 'tis in Europe countered a reproach—
> Where man asks questions for which man was made.
> A land without nobility, or wigs, or debt.
> No castles, no cathedrals, and no kings;
> Land of the forest.

There never was a titled aristocracy in America, though there are now economic and political elites and that fact, that we never had kings and hereditary nobility, has played an important part in the development of American national character. Most countries now, I would add, have, in theory at least, an egalitarian national ethos.

### Dumont on Indian Culture

India, on the other hand, represents a country where hierarchy, in the form of the caste system and the *jati*, is the dominant organizing principle of life and shapes people's lives from the moment they are born until they die—with rare exception. In a review-essay of Louis Dumont's book on India, *Homo Hierarchus* that appeared in her book *Implicit Meanings: Essays in Anthropology* (1975), the distinguished British social anthropologist Mary Douglas, discusses Dumont's ideas. She writes in her chapter titled "Louis Dumont's Structural Analysis":

> Professor Dumont presents India as a mirror image to ourselves: a society founded on principles exactly antithetical to those we honour.

> Our civilization is based on the premise of equality. The claims we make against one another are made in its name. . . . But in India the principle of social inequality is formally recognized as governing all social relations. The scale of hierarchy is set up on well-known rules. Contingent pressures from the actual distribution of wealth and power tend inevitably to distort their application. Our social pattern is reversed by their taking for principle what we take for contingency, and vice versa.

Dumont describes the two essential characteristics of Hindu society as, first, one in which status is determined by principles that are not based on the distribution of authority, and second, the importance of purity. Professor Douglas has done important work on the matter of attitudes towards purity and how these attitudes affect people in different cultures.

In Hinduism, she points out, the purity rules are all systematized into an intelligible set:

> Enormous pains are taken to control who eats what and who is served food by whom. The foods also are subject to the same principles of evaluation as occupations. Some are more grossly organic than others: the juice of vegetables does not contaminate as does the blood of animals; the veneration of the cow means that its products are pure, but anyone who eats beef is impure. (pp. 186-187)

The rules involving food, she adds, are so important a part of India culture that anthropologists have devoted more time to this subject than they have for food rules in Western countries.

The Hindu caste system, she adds, is able to absorb alien elements by applying its universal ranking rules of their purity code and separating off anything it deems impure. Then she raises an important issue, involving hierarchies found in Western societies:

> It is difficult to argue that stratification according to wealth and authority is less or more ruthless as a way of exploiting human beings than is stratification by scale-ranking according to purity rules. Rather the sheer political ineffectualness of the system in which purity rules dominate guarantees that those at the bottom of the scale will be short of material things and insecure of life and limb. (189)

Thus we find two hierarchical systems at work: one, in the West, is based on wealth and power and one, in India, is based on purity rules.

Dumont's argument is that human beings are, by nature, hierarchical and that wherever an egalitarian society is created, sooner or later hierarchy will become dominant. We must take this factor into account, he argues, when we make laws and institutions instead of blindly assuming that humans are, by nature, egalitarians. Once you recognize the hierarchical nature of human beings, Dumont suggests, you can then create institutions to deal with needs people and societies have. It is the categories of thought that people have that ultimately shape their societies and Dumont's book, Douglas argues, makes us consider the degree to which socially dominant categories of thought, such as those found in Western societies or in India, affect individual perceptions and social institutions.

It is possible to show the differences between American and India culture in the chart below. It is a bit reductionistic and pushes things to extremes in some cases, but it gives a good idea of how these two countries and cultures differ.

## Table 3.1
## America and India as Polar Opposites

| USA | India |
|---|---|
| egalitarian | hierarchical |
| class: money | caste: purity |
| young country | old country |
| old nation | young nation |
| without history | full of history |
| no hereditary aristocracy | hereditary aristocracy |
| achievement | ascription |
| "classless" all middle class | large middle class, huge peasantry |

## The Impact of Globalization and New Technologies

What Hindu India faces now, in an age in which globalization is becoming dominant, is a threat to its age-old rules of purity and ways of classifying people and shaping life. People in India can see what life is like in other countries and in other parts of India, where traditions may be weak or not followed at all. As first world popular culture and mass media become more widespread, the western value system will confront the caste system and it is very likely that large numbers of people will no longer be guided by it. In the large India cities, this is already occurring. In these cities, consumer cultures are developing and smashing ancient traditions.

That means that foreign tourists in India will probably be exposed to varying degrees of the weakening of the caste system and all that it entails and will be visiting an India that is in a profound state of transition between the old Hindu ways and new Western ways. In many cities, modern, Westernized Indians live quite differently from Indians in remote provinces. As the writer of one of my guidebooks wrote, when you leave Delhi and go into Rajasthan, you are going back in time. The question we must ask as we think about how India is evolving is—how long will it take Rajasthan to catch up to Delhi and the rest of the world? We might also wonder, does everyone there want to do so?

> A school textbook in western Rajasthan state compares housewives with donkeys and say the animals are more loyal and make better companions, the *Times of India* reported. The book was approved by the state's governing Hindu nationalist Bharatiya Janata Party and has set off protests by the party's women.
>
> Reuters. Quoted in Wednesday, April 5, 2006
> *New York Times*
> Page A10.

# 4

# Grid-Group Tourism and India

*The relation between social organization and values and beliefs can be demonstrated by an impressionistic exercise in grid/group analysis. This a way of checking characteristics of social organization with features of the beliefs and values of the people who are keeping the form of organization alive. Group means the outside boundary that people have erected between themselves and the outside world. Grid means all the other social distinctions and delegations of authority that they use to limit how people behave to one another. A society characterized by hierarchy would have many group-encircling and group-identifying regulations plus many grid constraints on how to act. An individualistic society would leave to individuals maximum freedom to negotiate with each other, so it would have no effective group boundaries and no insulating constrains on private dealings. A sectarian society [egalitarian] would be recognizable by strong barriers identifying and separating the community from nonmembers, but it would be so egalitarian that it would have no leaders and no rules of precedence or protocol telling people how to behave.*

—Mary Douglas and Aaron Wildavsky, *Risk and Culture*

This title of this chapter is a play on words, incorporating both social anthropologist Mary Douglas' Grid-Group theory and a very popular form of mass tourism, Group Tourism, in which numbers of people, who do not necessarily know one another, arrange to take a tour together. I will offer now a sociological, or more correctly, social anthropological analysis of how people make decisions about tourism choices—where to go and with whom—and a semiotic analysis of what tourists do. I could have used the title "Grid-Group Theory and Tourism" but it doesn't have the impact that "Grid-Group Tourism" has.

My focus will be on my decision to travel to Rajasthan and the way people decide where to go and what kind of arrangements they make when touring. It would seem to be a purely personal matter but there is reason to suggest that our decisions about where to travel are not just based on our interests and personalities.

## Grid Group Theory and Tourism

Let me start with Grid-Group theory, as elaborated by Mary Douglas and used by social scientists Aaron Wildavsky (who collaborated with Douglas on the book on risk quoted at the beginning of this chapter), Michael Thompson, and Richard Ellis. In their book *Cultural Theory* (1990), Thompson, Ellis, and Wildavsky explain Grid-Group theory:

> Our theory has a specific point of departure: the grid-group typology proposed by Mary Douglas. She argues that the variability of an individual's involvement in social life can be adequately captured by two dimensions of sociality: group and grid. *Group* refers to the extent to which an individual is incorporated into bounded units. The greater the incorporation, the more individual choice is subject to group determination. *Grid* denotes the degree to which an individual's life is circumscribed by externally imposed prescriptions. The more binding and extensive the scope of the prescriptions, the less of life that is open to individual negotiation. (5)

If you consider that there can be strong and weak group affiliation and few or many rules and prescriptions, you arrive at four "lifestyles," a term Douglas uses.

In an essay titled "Conditions for a Pluralist Democracy, or, Cultural Pluralism means More than One Political Culture," Aaron Wildavsky offers another way of considering Grid-Group theory (Berger, 2000):

> What matters to people is how they should live with other people. The great questions of social life are "Who am I?" (To what kind of a group do I belong?) and "What should I do?" (Are there many or few prescriptions I am expected to obey?). Groups are strong or weak according to whether they have boundaries separating them from others. Decisions are taken either for the group as a whole (strong boundaries)) or for individuals or families (weak boundaries). Prescriptions are few or many indicating that the individual internalizes a large or small number of behavioral norms to which or she is bound. By combining boundaries with prescriptions...the most general answers to the questions of social life can be combined to form four different political cultures. (7)

Wildavsky was writing about political cultures but I prefer to use the term Douglas used, "lifestyles," to explain Grid-Group theory. By taking the two dimensions discussed above, group membership (strong or weak) and grid aspects (few or many rules and prescriptions) we arrive at four lifestyles.

Wildavsky and Douglas differ in slight ways in terms of the names of these political cultures of lifestyles but the important point is that there are four lifestyles (there is actually a fifth but it is not relevant to our concerns) and these lifestyles play an important role in our decision making about political choices or tourism destinations.

Table 3.2
The Four Lifestyles

| Lifestyle | Group Boundaries | Number and Character of Rules |
|---|---|---|
| *Hierarchist* | Strong | Varied and numerous |
| *Fatalist* | Weak | Varied and numerous |
| *Egalitarian* | Strong | Few |
| *Individualist* | Weak | Few |

Thompson and his colleagues suggested that the hierarchist (sometimes called hierarchical elitist) and individualist lifestyles are the dominant ones in any society, with the egalitarians functioning as social critics who wish to help the fatalists, those at the bottom of the totem pole, rise from their lowly status.

In *Cultural Theory,* Thompson, Ellis, and Wildavsky explain:

> The alliance of individualism and hierarchy may be called, in current parlance, "the establishment." From this mixed-motive coalition individualists gain stability in property relationships and defense against outsiders, while hierarchy receives the enhanced economic growth pay off its promises to future generations. (88)

Egalitarians focus on the needs that all people have. Hierarchists believe in the importance of stratification, but have a sense of obligation to those below them. Individualists wish to be left alone to pursue their own interests with as little interference from the government or anyone else as possible. These four lifestyles are important because, as Douglas argues, they shape our consumption behavior.

In an essay titled "In Defence of Shopping," Douglas (1997) suggests that culture is really the arbiter of taste and that these four lifestyles, without our being aware of their role in our thinking, shape our consumption practices. And the most important aspect of consumption, for our purposes here, is that involving travel choices and tourism. She argues that

> consumption behavior is continuously and pervasively inspired by cultural hostility.... We have to make a radical shift away from thinking about consumption as a manifestation of individual choices. Culture itself if the result of myriads of individual choices, not primarily between commodities but between kinds of relationships. The basic choice that a rational individual has to make is the choice of what kind of society to live in. According to that choice, the rest follows. Artefacts are selected to demonstrate the choice. Food is eaten, clothes are worn, music, holidays, all the rest are choices that conform with the initial choice... (pp. 17-18)

That is, once we become a member of or identify with one of the four lifestyles, and the process is not one that we are usually aware of, we find ourselves rejecting the other three lifestyles and our consumption choices, in this particular case as they relate to holidays, are guided by that feeling of hostility.

All four lifestyles are in competition with one another and mutual hostility is the glue that holds societies together. As Douglas explains, "cultural alignment is the strongest predictor of preferences in a wide variety of fields" (23). She concludes her essay writing:

> Shopping is agonistic, a struggle to define not what one is, but what one is not. When we include not one cultural bias but four, and when we allow that each is bringing its critique against the others and when we see that the shopper is adopting postures of cultural defiance, that it all makes sense. (30)

Grid-Group theory suggests that when it comes to travel, our choices of destinations, tours to take, or ways of touring are based upon which of the four lifestyles we belong to and upon our desire to avoid being with those in other lifestyles. "Birds of a feather flock together," and tourists in one lifestyle, though they aren't necessarily conscious of the role their membership in a lifestyle is playing in shaping their choice of countries to visit and tours to take, try to avoid being with people from other lifestyles when they travel.

## Grid-Group Theory and Tourism Typologies

Earlier, I discussed the tourism typology of Erik Cohen who categorizes tourists as follows:

Organized Mass Tourists (in Group Inclusive Tours)
Individual Mass Tourists
Explorers (They plan their own itineraries)
Drifters and Backpacker types

Cohen uses the term "tourist bubble" to describe the experience of most Organized Mass Tourists. When they travel to third world countries, they enjoy first world comforts in expensive hotels and their experience with people in the countries they visit is usually highly sanitized.

I recently spent a month in Rajasthan and found that even though my wife and I wanted to walk around and interact with people in India, the traffic in some of the cities we visited was so chaotic and the nature of the stores so limited and uninteresting, that we were more or less forced, most of the time, to live in a tourist bubble—except that we stayed in three-star hotels that often had middle-class Indian tourists. In a few smaller cities we were able to walk around and purchase some souvenirs, but generally speaking, we were confined to our hotels and the sites of tourist interest and shops that our driver and guides took us to see.

The other important classification (and one widely cited in tourism scholarship) that I dealt with comes from Stanley Plog who sees tourists falling into two opposing categories—psychocentric or passive and allocentric or active, with most tourists falling in between these two polarities.

**Psychocentric** (passive)
Near-Psychocentric
Mid-Centric
Near Allocentric
**Allocentric** (active)

Tourists who travel in group tours and are driven around from place to place, descending from a bus to take photographs or dine together at a restaurant, are in Plog's typology psychocentric or near psychocentric. Tourists to Rajasthan would probably fit under his allocentric or near allocentric categories.

**Figure 4.1
A Typical Jain Temple**

To these well-known typologies we can now add another one, based upon Mary Douglas' Grid-Group lifestyles theory:

Hierarchists (sometimes called hierarchical elitists)
Individualists
Egalitarians (Douglas calls them enclavists)
Fatalists (Douglas calls them isolates)

According to Douglas' theory, tourists who belong to each of these lifestyles wish to avoid members of other lifestyles when they travel, and seek to find ways to be with members of their own lifestyle.

What complicates matters is that except for Fatalists, who are generally stuck where they are and don't have the resources to travel abroad, people can move from one lifestyle to another, so their travel choices may reflect their membership in one lifestyle or their aspirations or decisions to attach themselves to a different lifestyle. We will assume, however, to simplify matters, that the members of each lifestyle are content where they are and that their travel plans are connected to their membership in a given lifestyle and desire to avoid members of different lifestyles.

How people arrange to avoid members of other lifestyles and travel with people like themselves is an interesting question. Another way to phrase this is in the form of a question: how do tourists in each lifestyle find ways to maintain social distance from tourists from other lifestyles? In my travels in Rajasthan, my wife and I were dining in a little restaurant (recommended by *Lonely Planet India*) and noticed a sign. The restaurant had four rooms for travelers, available for three or four hundred rupees a night. So in India there are hotels that cost three hundred rupees a night (about six dollars) and others, like the super-deluxe six-star Oberoi hotels, which cost six hundred dollars a night.

Obviously, tourists who stay in hotels that cost six dollars a night are different from those who stay in hotels that cost six hundred dollars a night, so the cost of hotels and tours is one way that people can try to be with members of their own lifestyles. The hotel happened to be occupied by four backpacking couples from the Netherlands that night. The owner of the restaurant and hotel, who told us "think of this place as your home," informed me of this fact and said it was the first time everyone in his small hotel came from the Netherlands.

Tourists can also obtain social distance on cruises, with a wide variety of prices for cruises on different cruise lines. People who cruise on Silversea Lines are quite different from those who cruise on Carnival

Lines. Also, there is the matter of destinations, though tourists from each lifestyle face the problem of tourists from other lifestyles being attracted to certain "hot" destinations. In Agra, where the Taj Majal is the major tourist attraction, this social distance is maintained, to some degree, by the choice of hotel one stays in: Oberoi, at the top, and any number of no star, one-, two-, three-, and four-star hotels beneath it.

Tourists may act as they please but, if Douglas and other Grid-Group theorists are correct, they cannot please as they please. What pleases them, according to Douglas and other Grid-Group theorists, is based on the unconscious imperatives of the lifestyles to which they adhere and their negative feelings towards other competing lifestyles. There is a certain amount of freedom we all have since there is the possibility for many people to identify with different lifestyles, but we are all prisoners, to varying degrees, of the taste and stylistic consumption demands of our lifestyles.

# Part 2

## Semiotic Rajasthan

# 5

# Semiotics and Tourism

*The most important discovery of the first semiotic, that of Charles Peirce and Ferdinand de Saussure, was the principle of the arbitrariness of the relationship between the signifier and the signified. The example most often cited as illustration of this principle is the absence of natural connections between the sound of a word such as "tree" and the object it signifies. This is especially evident when words from different languages that mean the same things (tree, arbre, Baum) are compared. In the "Introduction" to a forthcoming book, Peter K. Manning provides some interesting nonlinguistic illustrations of the arbitrariness of the sign:*

> *The association between the wide-brimmed hat and cultural values of the land-owning haciendados in Anadalusia . . . between orchids and casting of spells to rid persons of evil or bodily afflictions . . . between types of grain and connotations of wealth, purity or spatial locale . . . are symbolic and can be understood only by unraveling the system of signs in which these associations become unquestioned.*

*The world of tourism is crowded with similar relationships: the connection between liberty and the Statue of Liberty is a monumental example.*

—Dean MacCannell, *The Tourist*

Regardless of the lifestyle to which tourists belong and the destinations tourists choose to visit, tourism can be understood, without being too reductionistic, as essentially semiotic in nature. In his book, *The Tourist: A New Theory of the Leisure Class* (1976), Dean MacCannell writes that "tourist attractions are signs" (109) and suggests that when tourists visit cities they don't "see" the city but only parts of it of touristic interest. He writes:

> Sightseers do not, in any empirical sense, *see* San Francisco. They see Fisherman's Wharf, a cable car, the Golden Gate Bridge, Union Square, Coit Tower, the Presidio, City Lights Bookstore, Chinatown, and perhaps the Haight-Ashbury or a nude go-go dancer in a North Beach-Barbary Coast club.

What he has listed are sights of semiotic interest that a typical tourist in San Francisco might see, but, as he explains, they never *see* San Francisco, just as tourists never *see* anyplace they go as a totality.

A useful bridge between Douglas' Grid-Group theory and semiotic theory comes from her statement that consumption involves an attempt to define not what one is but what one is not. This statement is very similar to one by Ferdinand de Saussure, one of the founding fathers of semiotics, who, wrote in his book *Course in General Linguistics* (1966) that "Concepts are purely differential and defined not by their positive content but negatively, by their relations with other terms of the system" (117). That is, concepts and derive their meaning, in essence, from being the opposite of other concepts.

Tourists are, for the most part, interested in visiting places that are different from their everyday worlds—places where they can satisfy their curiosity about how people live and obtain various other gratifications.

### A Very Brief Primer on Semiotic Theory

Let me offer a primer on semiotic theory here. It is an extremely complicated subject and there are an endless number of books dealing with semiotic theory and the applications of semiotics to everything under the sun. There are two founding fathers of the science of semiotics, which means, literally, the science of signs. Semiotics is concerned with how we find meaning in things. Ferdinand de Saussure, a Swiss linguistics professor, called his science *semiology*—literally words about signs-- but the term semiotics has become the term most often used. He said signs are made up of two components: a *signifier* (sound or object) and a *signified* (concept).

They are like two sides of a piece of paper. What is important to recognize is that the relationship between a signifier and signified is arbitrary and based on conventions. So signs often change their meaning.

Charles Sanders Peirce, who used the term *semiotics*, said there are three kinds of signs:

*Icons,* which signify by resemblance: a photo.

*Indexes,* which signify by cause and effect: smoke and a fire.

*Symbols,* which have to be learned: a cross, a flag, etc.

These terms are used in Peirce's statement that:

An analysis of the essence of a sign . . . leads to a proof that every sign is determined by its object, either first, by partaking in the characters of the object, when I call the sign an *Icon;* secondly, by being really and in its individual existence connected with the individual object, when I call the sign an *Index;* thirdly, by more or less approximating the certainty that it will be interpreted as denoting the object, in consequence of a habit (which term I use as including a natural disposition), when I call the sign a *Symbol.* (Quoted in J. Jay Zeman, "Peirce's Theory of Signs" in T. Sebeok, *A Perfusion of Signs,* 1977:36)

Peirce explained that a sign "is something which stands to somebody for something in some respect or capacity" (Zeman, 1977:27) and argued that the universe is, in essence, composed of signs. The "somebodies" in Peirce's quotation are tourists and the "somethings" represents places tourists visit and experiences they have when they travel.

From a semiotic perspective, tourists are people who seek out what semioticians describe as significant or in some cases iconic signs—that is, cathedrals, castles, museums, forts, and other buildings and sites of historic or aesthetic significance to experience them and generally speaking photograph or videotape them. To this list we can add foods, clothing, entertainments, and other aspects of everyday life found in foreign lands that provide new experiences and, in many cases, "photo opportunities." There are many different kinds of tourism, such as cultural tourism, adventure tourism, sex tourism, medical tourism, food tourism, drug tourism, and disaster tourism, and many tourists travel to satisfy more than one desire.

One of the most interesting semiotic analysis of a foreign country was done by the French semiotician Roland Barthes, who wrote a book about Japan titled *Empire of Signs*. In this book he deals with Japanese signs such as pachinko, chopsticks, bowing, the Japanese eyelid, sukiyaki, and other phenomena or signs that interested him. He pointed out that he wasn't trying to "photograph" Japan, by which he meant offer a complete and systematic portrait of Japan. Instead, he was interested in certain things that caught his eye, what he called "flashes."

From a semiotic perspective, then, the world is full of signs and tourism is a means of seeking out and experiencing signs in different places. Semiotics is an imperialistic science. Everything can be analyzed semiotically: facial expressions, hair styles, body ornaments, foods, clothing, space, architecture, and so on. They are all signifiers that have to be probed for what they signify.

The term "sightseeing" can be understood, from a semiotic perspective, as "sign-seeing," since sites are signs. We take photographs of the places we visit as a way of remembering our trips and proof that we actually went to the places we photograph. That is why many tourists take photographs showing them standing in front of some famous building or other place of touristic importance.

## Semiotics and the Tourist Imagination

I suggested earlier that there are three stages that tourists generally go through in traveling to foreign countries. They do this by taking a tour or finding some other way to see the important sights in a foreign country that they've never visited before. I will take, as a case study, Rajasthan, India, which my wife and I recently visited. Some tourists may make "last-minute" snap decisions and decide to go to some foreign country just a few days before they leave, but this kind of travel is the exception, not the rule. In the case of India, tourists from the United States need a visa, so it is unlikely that they make quick decisions about traveling there.

*Stage 1: The Imagined Place*

Before I went to India, I read a number of books and magazine articles on India and looked over information on Frommer's "Travel Talk" website about India. One issue of the *National Geographic Traveler* had a sixty-page spread on India and *Time* magazine had a cover image and long article about India.

*Stage 2: The Actual Visit*

This stage involves our actual trip. "Nothing can prepare you for India," someone said to me recently, and he was correct. Our visit to India was wonderful in many respects, but travel in India is difficult and demanding because of the lack of infrastructure. Even though some of our trips between cities were only two hundred kilometers, it generally took many hours to get from one place to another. So we spent a great deal of time in a car, looking at the scenery, as our driver miraculously weaved between huge trucks, cattle, and buffalo wandering on roads, flocks of sheep, herds of goats, stray dogs, tuk-tuks, and pedestrians.

In the course of twenty-five days in India, my wife and I were at twelve hotels and visited most of the touristically "important" places in Rajasthan. Some of the hotels were absolutely wonderful but a couple of them were not too pleasant to be in. As I mentioned earlier, many Indian companies offer tours of Rajasthan and they are all pretty similar in terms of the places they go. They differ in terms of the hotels they use and the kind of cars they use. Thus, anyone who visits Rajasthan probably will find themselves also taking a side-trip to Agra to visit the Taj Mahal, either at the start of the tour or at its end.

During my visit, being a good tourist, I took 250 photographs with my digital camera and my wife took another 100 or so photographs. And we bought a small rug and some inexpensive items such as pillow covers and napkins, all of which were quite beautiful. I bought myself a pair of jooti slippers, made of camel skin, for five dollars.

*Stage 3: The Remembered Tour*

This stage takes place after you've visited a country and are back home. In this stage there is a tendency either to forget about some of the negative aspects of the trip or to recall them in great detail. People often ask you about your trip, especially when it was in an exotic and distant land like India, and you have to offer a capsule description of your adventures, good and bad.

The digital camera plays a role in this stage. In my case, I downloaded my images into my computer and put them in Picasa and now, when I pause in keyboarding for two minutes, images of India start showing up on my monitor in fairly rapid succession. These images enable me to remember the trip and recall some of the fantastic places we visited and delightful (and, in a few cases, not so pleasant) experiences we had.

Like many tourists, I also kept a journal and so I have notes written every day about our experiences and my impressions of India. Since I went to India with the idea of writing a book about tourism in Rajasthan, I wrote a great deal and spent a lot of energy looking for Rajasthani signs that I could interpret. My problem was finding signs that reflected Rajasthani culture, and in some cases, Indian culture.

## Problems Tourist Face

Tourists don't realize they are engaged in a semiotic activity. Most people outside of academia have never heard the term "semiotics," but that doesn't mean that they aren't functioning as semioticians. The fact that they take so many photographs (icons in Peirce's trichotomy) proves the point. But tourists face certain problems relative to signs.

First, there is the matter of information overload or perhaps image overload may be more correct. There are so many new experiences, so many forts and castles and palaces and other things to see and to photograph in Rajasthan that one's mind becomes somewhat dazed. On a half-hour boat trip on the lake in Udaipur, a tourist sitting in front of me must have taken fifty photographs. If you have a digital camera with a one-gigabite compact flash card in it, you can take five hundred high-quality images and with a two gigabite card you can take a thousand high-resolution images. You can delete any of the images you don't like afterwards, but having a digital camera encourages people to take large number of photographs.

Second, there is the matter of tourist traps and "fake" sites, designed to give tourists a false idea of life in the country being visited. Tourists are usually searching for the exotic and the authentic but too often what they get is the pseudo-authentic that offer kitschy staged experiences based on stereotyped notions some travelers have. In some cases, tourism companies collude with tourist traps to give tourists the stereotyped experiences they are looking for. As the novelist and semiotician Umberto Eco pointed out, if signs can tell the truth, they can also lie. In fact, if they can't lie, they can't tell the truth. So signs are slippery phenomena.

Third, there are any number of scams to which tourists are susceptible. On our tour, many of our guides (we had different guides in each city) suggested we visit a shop owned by a cousin or uncle where we would get a good price or that we visit a government-sponsored shop that helped poor people sell their goods. When you purchase something at a shop to which your guide brings you, you generally end up paying more for the item, since the guide invariably gets a commission. We dealt with this problem, most of the time, by going on our own to real government shops with fixed prices.

Let me now offer, in the chapter that follows, a semiotic analysis and interpretation of various aspects of Rajasthani culture that the typical tourist experiences while traveling there. India is a huge nation, with many different states, each of which has its own languages, cuisines, styles of dress, and so on. But they all are part of India and thus have some things in common. So in writing about Rajasthan I'm also writing about India. My focus is upon Rajasthan but much of what I write also applies to Indian life in general. This is analogous to writing about California or the Pacific Northwest or New England or the Deep South. There are regional variations on American life of considerable magnitude yet, at the same time, certain things Americans have in common.

# 6

# A Semiotic Perspective of Rajasthan (and the Golden Triangle)

*Of all the world's countries, India is the most truly prodigious, and this quality of astonishment displays itself afresh every day as the sun comes up in Delhi . . . cities as vast as Bombay and Calcutta, villages so lost in time that no map marks them, nuclear scientists and aboriginal hillmen, industrialists of incalculable wealth and dying beggars sprawled on railway platforms . . . an inexhaustible history, an incomprehensible social system, an unfathomable repository of human resource, misery, ambiguity, vitality and confusion—all this, the colossal corpus of India, invests, sprawls around, infuses, elevates, inspires and very nearly overwhelms New Delhi.*

—Jan Morris, *Destinations*

In this chapter I analyze important sites and aspects of Rajasthani (and Indian) life and culture, with some additional comments on the Taj Mahal, which is part of the "Golden Triangle," but is in Uttar Pradesh and not Rajasthan. I start with the flag of India, which is very important from a symbolic perspective and encapsulates, one may say, the polar oppositions and often hidden tensions between Hindus and Muslims that inform life in India. I will then discuss the Taj Mahal, which is often the first stop beyond Delhi that many tourists make as they begin their tours of India, and then I move on to other iconic signs and subjects of interest.

## The Indian Flag and the Religious Divide

The Indian flag, which was adopted when India became independent in 1947, has three horizontal strips of equal size: orange on the top, white in the middle, and green on the bottom. In the middle of the white stripe there is a navy blue wheel with twenty-four spikes that is three quarters the height of the white stripe. These colors, a guide told me, are tied to religions in India. The orange stripe represents Hinduism, the green stripe represents Islam, and the white stripe represents all the other "minor" religions in India, of which there are many.

The population in India is divided between Hindus (80.5 percent), Muslims (16.5 percent), and the rest for the other religions. These statistics indicate that there are around 175 million Muslims in India, which makes India home to the largest number of Muslims of any country except for Indonesia. The two religions, Hinduism and Islam, differ in a number of ways and they are, it turns out, polar opposites in many important aspects of their core beliefs. There is a continual tension between these two religions that affects and shapes much of Indian culture and society and everyday life.

In the *Insight Guide to India,* edited by Andrew Eames, V.S. Naravane has written a chapter on "The Religions of India" and deals with the various oppositions one finds in the two religions (1997:91):

> Unlike Hinduism, Islam was founded by a historical person and has a specific scripture. Hinduism is eclectic and pluralistic; Islam is homogenous and has a definite concept of God. Hinduism has the luxuriance of the tropical forests and river valleys; Islam has the simplicity and austerity of the desert. The Hindu temple is closed on three sides, and there is an air of mystery in the dark inner sanctum; the Muslim mosque is open on all sides, exposed to light and air. The Hindu worships sculptured images of deities; to the Muslim, idol-worship is the most grievous of sins.

Navarane adds that Hinduism is not a proselytizing religion while Muslims regard converting non-Muslims as meritorious. Somehow, though, the two religions, so different, have found a way to accommodate and enrich each other.

To make it easier to see the polar oppositions between these two religions, I will construct a chart showing the oppositions discussed by Naravane and add some others which guides and others told me about. Some of these polarities might be a bit stretched but they do a good job, I believe, of highlighting the important differences between the two religions in India.

There is, then, a huge chasm that exists between the two religions and though the people of India generally manage to live in a state of relative harmony, there is always an undercurrent of tension that occasionally flares up into violent religious confrontations. How ironic it is, then, that the most iconic building in India, and a building that is generally listed in the "top ten" iconic buildings in the world, is a Muslim one—the Taj Mahal, the subject of my next analysis.

## The Taj Mahal

At a dinner party I attended shortly after returning from India, I got into a conversation with a woman who had been to India a number of

# A Semiotic Perspective of Rajasthan (and the Golden Triangle)

**Table 6.1**
**Hinduism and Islam Polarities**

| Hinduism | Islam |
|---|---|
| Orange color | Green color |
| Many founders | Founded by a historical person |
| Numerous religious texts | Koran: one all-important scripture |
| Many gods worshiped | One god worshiped |
| Worship sculptured images | Idol worship forbidden |
| Temples enclosed on three sides | Mosques open on all sides |
| Round domes on temples | Pointy domes on temples |
| Tropical forests and river valleys | The desert |
| Exclusionary: shun proselytizing | Inclusive: Favor proselytizing |
| Solar | Lunar |
| Vegetarians | Meat eaters (but no pork) |
| Palms down when they pray | Palms up when they pray |
| Mustaches point up | Mustaches point down |
| Caste system | No castes |

**Figure 6.1**
**Thatched Huts at the Resort Rawla in the Thar Desert**

**Figure 6.2**
**Doorman at the Holiday Inn in Jaipur**

years ago. "I only went to India," she said, "because I wanted to see the Taj Mahal. And I've been to India twice, just so I could see the Taj Mahal. I remember when I first saw it. I stood mesmerized by it, unable to take my eyes off it, almost hypnotized by its unbelievable beauty." There have been many superlatives written about this building. The poet Rabindranath Tagore described it as a "teardrop on the face of eternity."

These views contrasted with the description of the Taj Mahal by a friend, a former editor of mine, who told me he had been to India and seen the Taj Mahal. "What did you think of it?" I asked? "It's a big white building," he replied. This description suggests he was not willing to be taken in by all the hype about the building.

**Figure 6.3
The Celebrated Taj Mahal in Agra**

Going to see the Taj Mahal involves a number of steps. You drive to a parking lot and there you take a battery-operated vehicle for a five minute ride to the area where the Taj Mahal is located. When you buy your ticket to see the Taj Mahal, you are given a small bottle of water and plastic coverings for your shoes. You aren't allowed bring in food, tripods, and various other articles. Once you've bought your ticket and been admitted to the grounds, you pass through a large building and finally get to see the Taj Mahal and other buildings that are part of the complex.

The electric vehicles are used to prevent pollution from damaging the building. Our guide told us that all new manufacturing plants had been moved to the outskirts of Agra, to cut down on pollution and acid rain—but that night, when I went to the roof of our hotel, which had a viewing area, you could hardly see the Taj Mahal because of the pollution. My hotel was a kilometer away from the Taj Mahal.

The workmanship in the building is incredible, with remarkably delicate marble screens and other carvings, and many inlaid jewels. The Taj Mahal is a very beautiful building and a remarkable one, as well. The question in my mind is how much of the appeal of the building is due to all the material about it generated by writers and journalists, and the history or "back story" connected with it, and how much is due to its intrinsic beauty? There are many other very beautiful buildings in India, and in other countries as well, but few have the aura of the Taj Mahal and the capacity to generate the kinds of feelings found in many who visit it. As the author of *Lonely Planet India* writes (2005:357) "As an architectural masterpiece, it stands head and shoulders above any other contenders."

Part of the mystique of the Taj Mahal is its history. It was built as a memorial by Emperor Shah Jahan for his second wife, Mumtaz Mahal, who died in 1631 giving birth to their fourteenth child. Shah Jahan was the grandson of the emperor Akbar. According to the legend, Sha Jahan was so distraught by the death of Mumtaz that his hair turned white overnight. He started building the mausoleum in 1631 and finished it in 1653. So it took more than twenty years to build and required twenty-thousand workers to complete it, at a cost, in today's money, of around seventy million American dollars. The Taj Mahal is a UNESCO World Heritage Site. It is built on a raised marble platform, which means when you see the Taj Mahal, it is always seen silhouetted against the sky. When the sun is out and the sky is blue, the white marble of the Taj Mahal glistens radiantly. Four minarets are on the corners of the area where the building is located. One is leaning slightly, which our guide said was God's way of showing human fallibility.

One of the pleasures of travel is what can be described as "time travel," going back to earlier times to see the wonders of the world. The Taj Mahal, finished in 1651, enables us to get a glimpse of what earlier architects and builders were capable of doing and to walk where once emperors and kings did and gaze upon the fruits of Shah Jahan's love. There is an ironic twist to this story. Shah Jahan's son, Aurangzeb overthrew his father in 1658 and imprisoned his father (under house arrest) in the Agra Fort, which Akbar had started in 1565, so Shan Jahan spent eight years, until his death, in a fort where he could look out over the Yamuna river, and see his beloved Taj Mahal, glistening in the sun. According to our guide, Aurangzeb did this because his father was planning to build another Taj Mahal, in black marble, on the other size of the Yamuna River and Aurangzeb thought this would bankrupt the city.

### The Palace of Winds (Hawa Mahal) in Jaipur

Jaipur is the main city in Rajasthan, and the second leg of the "Golden Triangle. Many tourists who arrive in Delhi book tours that include the

Golden Triangle: Delhi, Agra, and Jaipur. Some tourists go to Agra on the first leg of the Golden Triangle and some tourists go to Jaipur and then go to Agra on the way back to Delhi. Tourists who are taking long trips in Rajasthan often start in Jaipur and visit Agra and the Taj Mahal on the return leg of their travels. The Palace of Winds (Hawa Mahal) in Jaipur is also an iconic building and is shown in most tourism books about India or Rajasthan because of its beauty and because of its historical and cultural interest.

This building was erected in 1799 by Maharajah Sawai Pratep Singh. It is one of the most photographed buildings in Rajasthan and is probably Jaipur's most important symbol. The pink building, part of the City Palace complex, is an architectural curiosity, being five stories high but only one room deep at the top. It was built to enable women confined in the royal household to *purdah* to be able to observe the goings on in Jaipur.

The building, in reality little more than a facade of pink sandstone, has an amazing 953 windows. The top three stories of the building are one large room. We can get a sense of the importance of this building when we see that it is given a two-page color spread in the 1997 *Insight Guides India*. Obviously, the building has a great deal of significance as a symbol of Jaipur and Rajasthan. It is visually arresting and very beautiful. The question arises—why build a building five stories high and one story deep at the top? Why not build a larger building with many rooms, especially since there is a huge fort in Jaipur and there are many huge forts and castles and palaces in other cities Rajasthan?

The reason that is generally given is that by having a thin building, the winds could be used to cool it down, since they could blow through the building without being impeded. Another reason might be to isolate, as much as possible, the women in purdah, who used it to watch the daily activities in Jaipur. By having the building so small, the women in it could only use it for watching others and it could not have other major functions of any importance.

Even now, women in Rajasthan tend to be isolated. I noticed that we saw very few women working in the hotels where we stayed. All of the jobs were done by men, except that a couple of hotels, in larger cities, had women in the reception desks. But the waiters, room cleaners, and everyone else in the hotels we stayed at were men.

The Hawa Mahal is on a busy street in Jaipur and is surrounded by other buildings. It isn't given any room for display, to set it off from the adjoining buildings—it seems like just one more building in Jaipur that you may not even notice in passing, except that many tourists coming to

**Figure 6.4
The Palace of Winds in Jaipur**

Rajasthan will have seen photos of it in various guidebooks.. You have to take pictures of it from the sidewalk across the street, which is the only place you can get a good frontal view of it.

The maharajah who had it built, Maharajah Sawai Pratep Singh, was a remarkable person of legendary proportions. He has been described as being seven feet tall, four feet wide, and weighing 500 pounds. It seems rather strange that a gigantic man like this would have a delicate building like that Hawa Mahal built, but he "projected" his sense of power in other ways, namely the city palace.

### Rajasthani Mustaches

The quintessential male mustache in Rajasthan is very full with the tips turned up. You see these mustaches on many paintings and other images from the past, but modern Rajasthanis, an informant told me, now think it is more modern not to wear a mustache. The doorman at our first hotel in Jaipur, Rajasthan, wore a costume and had a very large and full Rajasthani mustache. Whenever we went in or out of the hotel, he opened the door and saluted, smartly, smiling and greeting us warmly. Our driver also had a Rajasthani mustache and felt an enormous sense of pride in it.

Once when we were stuck in traffic, two young men on a motorcycle who were beside our car said something to him. He rolled down the window to hear what they said more clearly and then replied to them.

"What did they say?" I asked.

"They told me how much they admire my mustache," he said.

Mustaches are a sign of masculinity and the large Rajasthani mustache can be considered a hypermasculine sign, reflecting a sense of male virility and of being connected to and identifying with the Rajah warriors of earlier days in Rajasthan, who wore these mustaches. In many countries it is common for men to wear mustaches of one sort or another to secure and solidify their male identity. A Rajasthani man wearing a bushy mustache carries on the long tradition of Rajasthani maharajahs and warriors. These Rajasthani mustaches are also a reflection of a certain kind of narcissism and exhibitionism—though these mustaches are still widespread enough so as to mute this aspect of mustaches to some degree. When I took a close-up picture of our driver, Roshan, so I could have a good example of a Rajasthani mustache for my photo collection, he was positively beaming.

The fact that mustaches are now "out of fashion" with many young men in Rajasthan suggests they are making an attempt to escape from the old ways and adopt modern lifestyles—perhaps as the result of the globalization and modernization that are having such a profound impact on Indian society and culture.

### The "Rat Temple" at Deshnok

The Karni Mata temple in Deshnok, thirty kilometers south of Bikaner, is, a guide told me, the only temple in India where rats are worshiped. Karni Mata, who was born in the fourteenth century, was a so-called "miracle worker" who is supposed to have gone into the underworld to plead for the life of her dead nephew. She was refused, so she is said to have told Yamraj, the god of death, that when her followers died, they would be reborn as *kaaba,* sacred rats, for a lifetime, and then be reborn as bards—denying him souls to rule over. Karni Mata was seen as an incarnation of the goddess of power, Durga.

The temple was built in the early 1900s by the Maharajah Ganga Singh and contains an estimated 20,000 rats. In the Hindu religion, there is a belief in the transmigration of souls, a cycle called Samsara, so the rats in the temple are seen by Hindus as reborn souls of people. It is considered a blessing by many Indians to eat food that has been covered with rat saliva and a sign of good luck to see a white rat. One of the treasures in

**Figure 6.5
Our Driver Roshan and His Rajasthani Mustache**

the temple are the solid silver carved doors in the sanctuary. An image on one of the doors shows the goddess Karni Mata, with bent, outstretched arms. She is standing on a short platform. There is a bird fluttering just above her left hand and sacred rats are shown scurrying around her feet. In her right hand she holds a trident. The sanctuary in the temple is off limits to people who are not Hindus.

To enter this temple, like all Hindu temples, you must take off your shoes and walk in a temple where rats are scurrying around and others are at huge saucers, around three feet in diameter, drinking milk. There are rat feces everywhere. It is an eerie feeling, walking in the temple. When I was there, the area in front of the sanctum was mobbed and I could only see a little bit of what was in the room, so I took a photograph over the heads of the throng of people in front of me, and left. We wore throwaway socks that we got on Singapore Airlines, which we deposited in a trash container outside of the temple. The rats in the temple are not huge sewer rats but a small variety—similar in size to the pet rat we got for our children when they were young.

In her book *In Rajasthan* (1997), Royina Grewal describes her experience being at the temple:

> We enter the courtyard... roofed with wire mesh to protect the *kaaba* from predators. I have had to remove my shoes, and am grateful for the thick socks that I remembered to put on in the morning. The *kaaba* are everywhere. My skin crawls as one scurried over my feet and Saini [a friend who took her to the temple] advises me to shuffle to avoid the dreadful sin of stepping on one. I stifle my squeamishness as I shuffle to the sanctum, where my attempts to focus on the shrine are distracted by the *kaaba* which are crawling everywhere. (pp. 227-228)

She describes the temple, full of rats lapping milk from a huge pot and eating a special kind of halwa that is made for them by devotees of the temple. She reminds us, though, that the temple is devoted to Karni Mata, not the holy rats, which are kept in the temple as a sanctuary. In her book, she mentions talking with a man about her forthcoming trip the temple. He cautioned her to watch where she walked because if she trampled a rat, he said, it could be his grandfather. The rats have a status in the temple as holy or sacred animals, which is just the opposite of the way people in most countries feel about rats.

When I was there, I saw a mother bring her two children over to watch the rats lapping up milk. They were all very excited about being in the temple with the rats. When rats are pets, we think about them differently than when they are wild pests and want to kill them, not give them sanctuary. It is easy to understand why Royina Grewal's skin "crawled" when one of them scurried over her foot; that is probably the way most foreign tourists in India would respond to a visit to this temple. It is, most certainly, one of the most curious and remarkable tourist sites in Rajasthan and, no doubt, in all of India.

### Tigers in Ranthambore National Park

Ranthambore is a tourist destination built on the fact that in the nature preserve there, one can—if lucky enough—take "tiger safaris" and see wild tigers. It is estimated that there are more than thirty of them living in the park and in recent years, a number of cubs have been born. The guide books suggest you arrange to go to the park three or four times if you hope to see a tiger. There are also crocodiles, monitor lizards, wild boars, and other wildlife in the park, which also contains ruins of temples, mosques, and an old fort. Tourists, both domestic and foreign, can find many hotels in Ranthanbore and a nearby city, Sawai Madhopur. The park has limited the number of jeeps and canters that are allowed in to help preserve it.

The use of the term "safaris" in Ranthambore National Park suggests that it offers an experience similar to what tourists to African countries experience but at a fraction of the cost. You can find very fine hotels in the area for less than one hundred dollars and many at ever lower prices. One of the reasons Rajasthan is such an important tourist destination is that it offers a number of different kinds of experiences—elephant rides in Jaipur, camel safaris in the Thar desert, and tiger safaris in Ranthambore National Park.

India is one of the few countries in Asia where there are still wild tigers, but their numbers are constantly being depleted because poachers kill them to sell their hides and various parts of them to people in China and other countries. So the tigers represent a battleground in which the Indian government and tourism companies are fighting against poachers. Without tigers the hotels in the area would be empty. When my wife and I visited stayed in Ranthambore, the park had been shut down for some reason and the hotels were empty. One night there were the only two couples in our hotel, which had around one hundred rooms. Tourism, then, plays an important, perhaps a pivotal, role in the battle to preserve wild tigers in India. The tiger is, I should add, the national animal of India, which explains why artists who want to represent India by an animal choose tigers.

Why does seeing a tiger in the wild matter to people so much? Tigers have a mystique about them and the chance to see them in the wild gives tourists the ability to "time travel" to periods in the past when tigers were abundant. Seeing wild tigers also provides striking and rare photo opportunities. Now tigers are an extremely precious resource and because their numbers are so small, seeing a wild tiger becomes a testimonial of sorts to tourists who have traveled far and seen what may be the remnants of a species that is gradually disappearing from wildernesses everywhere. Seeing a wild tiger now has become a privilege, available, generally speaking, only to tourists who spend a considerable amount of money for the chance to see one.

### Images of India in the *Economist*

"India Overheats." That is the main title on the cover of the February 3-9, 2007 issue of the *Economist,* which shows a highly stylized drawing of a tiger, in the jungle, with its tail on fire. The cover suggests that India is an animal that is dangerous, and one article suggests why. It begins:

> The Indian tiger is on the prowl. This week, in an apt piece of symbolism, Tata Steel, which dates back to the days of the Raj, leapt into the league of top producers when it

**Figure 6.6**
**Exterior of the Karni Mata Temple in Deshnok**

bought Britain's Corus, which includes the steelmaking remnants of the old imperial power. Nor is Tata alone: younger India companies such as Infosys and Wipro are storming international markets. (11)

What the tiger suggests is the predatory and dangerous aspects of India's new-found economic power, which the *Economist* suggests is in danger of overheating as it attempts to catch up with China and become a global economic power. The *Economist* estimates that with a growth rate of 9.2 percent, India may soon become the third largest economy, after the United States and China.

Later in the magazine there is an article on India's man-pulled rickshaws being outlawed in Kolkatta (Calcutta), another article on retailing, dealing with the development of supermarkets in India, and finally a more substantial article on India's economy titled "India on Fire." The illustration for that article shows an Indian dancer in an elaborate costume, and next to him is a hand holding a stick with a large fire illuminating the dancer.

In these articles we see the problems Westerners face in dealing with India, for it is hard to reconcile a country that has atom bombs, millions of highly trained engineers, an extremely high growth rate and, at the same time, has millions of cows wandering around its streets and millions of desperately poor farmers. Perhaps the feeling people get when trying to comprehend or make sense of India is best captured by the quotation above from the brilliant travel writer Jan Morris, namely that India confounds us. Trying to "comprehend" India, to make sense of it, is difficult, if not impossible for Westerners, for there is too much history in India, too many people, too many contradictions. The puzzlement we face in trying to get some kind of a grasp on Indian life and culture is also reflected in the famous description, in E. M. Forster's *A Passage to India* (1924), of Mrs. Moore in the Marabar cave:

> The echo in a Marabar cave is . . . is entirely devoid of distinction. Whatever is said, the same monotonous noise replies, and quivers up and down the walls until it is absorbed into the roof. "Boum" is the sound as far as the human alphabet can express it, or "bou-oum," or "ou-boum,"—utterly dull. Hope, politeness, the blowing of a nose, the squeak of a boot, all produce "boum." Even the striking of a match starts a little worm coiling, which is too small to complete a circle but it eternally watchful. (pp. 147-148)

The "boum" that Forster writes about is a good example of the difficulty that Westerners—maybe even many Indians—face in trying to understand certain aspects of Indian life and culture. What Forster wrote about the Marabar caves, that they "rob infinity and eternity of their vastness," can be said about Rajasthan and India.

Journalists who write about India may at times be completely missing the boat in their articles, because India's cultural complexities are so difficult to comprehend. I always feel that my analyses of Rajasthan and India must always be tempered with the realization that I may be making terrible mistakes, even though I try to be honest and to use my understanding of semiotic theory and my observations to shed some light on aspects of Indian culture that attracted my attention. On the other hand, writing as a "stranger" in a culture does alert one to certain important aspects of that culture that natives often neglect.

## Sacred Cows

In his book *Strange Lands and Friendly People,* published in 1951, William O. Douglas has a chapter on "Nehru's Welfare State." In this chapter he comments about India's famous "sacred cows":

> There are 257,000,000 cattle in India. Among these are dairy herds that compare favorably with the best; but most of them are thin and scrawny, their ribs plainly visible. Since the land can support only 60 per cent of the 257,000,000 cattle, there is not enough food to go around; consequently the cows give on the average only a quart of milk a day. Cows are sacred in Hindu religion. They may not be killed; the meat may not be eaten. And so hungry cattle get a bare subsistence on fodder that should go to humans. (302)

Douglas mentions that when he was visiting in Uttar Pradesh, the rumor that someone had killed a cow led to a riot and that the government's attempt to reduce the number of cows in India was halted. He recounts how an Indian politician gave a speech in which he said that maintaining Hindu religious principles was more important than economic prosperity.

Douglas is repeating a commonly held notion at the time—and one that some experts in Indian culture still hold—namely that the sacred cows in India are an economic burden and India would be much better off with fewer cows. As I will suggest, shortly, there are reasons to question this assumption and to assert that rather than being a burden, India's cows are a significant economic benefit. When the Hindu sages decided to make cows sacred a thousand years ago, they made—it has been argued—a very wise decision.

The fact that cows and buffalo are allowed to roam freely in Rajasthan and in India means India can be considered, in certain respects, a gigantic dairy farm and Indians are all, in a sense, dairy farmers, whatever else they may be. In the United States and most First World countries cows and other dairy animals are kept on farms and isolated from the general public. Not so in Rajasthan (and elsewhere in India), where both in big cities and small towns you see them, often standing immobile in the sides of roads for long periods of time, and then wandering around, often crossing roads and forcing traffic to stop or detour around them.

In my statistical portrait of India, I pointed out that there are an estimated four hundred million cows and buffalo in India. I've seen other figures that give the number of cows in India at two hundred million, with ninety million water buffalo. It is estimated that there are 1.5 billion cows in the world and that India has the largest number of cows of any country in the world. It has been estimated that India has between one-fourth and one-sixth of the world's cows, which are sacred animals there, and one half of the world's buffalo, which are not sacred and which are a better source of milk than cows.

There is a considerable amount of debate by anthropologists and other social scientists about these sacred cows. In economic terms, there is a question about whether cows are "cost-efficient," aside from the spiritual imperatives in the Hindu religion that provide a rationale for keeping them. India is a sacred society and because cows are seen as sacred, the Indians feel obligated to provide for them.

But it may also be that there are economic reasons that justify maintaining the huge number of cows and buffalo in India. They provide milk and require people to milk them, so the people of India and their cows are locked into a system in which each needs the other. But they also provide dung, which is used for a variety of purposes. Cow dung mixed with dirt makes a very hard concrete-like substance that is used for yards and in some buildings. Cow dung is also dried, made into little patties, and used for heating. So the cows do, in may ways, pay for themselves.

In an article on the Internet at the Indian Dairy Industry website, "The Sacred Cow!" (http:www.indiadairy.com/info_sacred_cow.html) we find some interesting data about the economic productivity of these sacred cows:

> A scientific study reported that the total efficiency of the "desi" (indigenous) cattle in terms of energy output amounts to 17 per cent as opposed to 4 per cent for the American Beef Cattle. The reason being the optimal utilization of all its products.

> According to the National Council of Applied Economic Research (NCAER), cattle dung in India has a fuel value equivalent to 35 million tones of wood. An estimated one-third of the dung, amounting to some 300 million tones, is used as fuel in rural houses. Another 340 million tones go back to the soil as organic fertilizer.

The site points out that the energy from seventy million bullocks, eight million buffalo, a million horses and another million camels is estimated at around 60,000 million kilowatts hours, with a value of from 60,000 to 100,000 million rupees. The article adds that animal power generates two thirds of the total energy used in India while other conventional sources generate only fourteen percent of India's energy needs. Cattle are, then, "thermal and chemical" factories.

Marvin Harris, an anthropologist, made a similar arguments in his book *Cows, Pigs, Wars and Witches: The Riddles of Culture* (1975). In his chapter "Mother Cow," he attacks the view of many experts, at that time, that India's worship of holy cows was the number one cause of poverty and hunger in India. These experts argued that it was senseless to keep a hundred million "useless" animals alive when so many people were hungry and starving.

Harris takes issue with this notion:

> A farmer who owns a cow owns a factory for making oxen. With or without cow love, there is a good reason for him not to be too anxious to sell his cow to the slaughterhouse. One also begins to see why Indian farmers might be willing to tolerate cows that give only 500 pounds of milk per year. If the main function of the zebu cow is to breed male traction animals, then there's no point in comparing her with specialized American dairy animals, whose main function is to produce milk. (16)

Harris adds that the milk the Indian cows produce plays a big role in feeding large numbers of people who live on the edge of starvation.

It is the female buffalo that are the major source of milk in India, and both are major sources of dung, which, as we've seen, has many uses

**Figure 6.7
Piles of Dried Cow Dung used for Heating**

in Indian culture, such as fertilizer and as a source of heat for cooking. So there is good reason to suggest that these cows, which one sees everywhere in India, have both a sacred significance and a practical utility and all those sacred cows play a major role in the Indian economy. As any traveler to India knows, when cows start to move across a road, all the traffic stops or weaves around them to let them go wherever they are heading.

## Elephants in Rajasthan and India

Like many tourists in Jaipur, we rode on elephants up the hill leading to the Amber fort there. You walk up steps to a tower that makes it easy for you to step onto the platform on the elephants back, and then the mahout guides the elephant up to the fort. The conventional tip for this ride is fifty or one hundred rupees. There are a limited number of elephants allowed to transport tourists so there are often long lines to get onto the elephants and if you don't get to the transport area in time, you take an elephants to the fort, but have to walk to it or go by automobile or some other means. In the afternoon you can see the elephants, in a long line on the side of the road, slowly trudging back to the area where they are kept. There is some question about how well they are treated and some animal rescue groups have raised questions about this matter.

Elephants have played a large role in Rajasthani history, since they were used in fighting for thousands of years and Rajasthan and Indian history is full of records of great battles between armies with huge numbers of war elephants. Elephants were the tanks of ancient military campaigns. But since elephants consume a great deal of food, the cost of supporting these elephants was staggering. It has been estimated that elephants consume between one hundred and forty to two hundred and seventy kilograms of food a day, which means it costs a good deal to maintain an elephant, and some maharajas and generals had herds of thousands of fighting elephants.

They were used in a battle between the ruler of Punjab, King Porus, and Alexander the Great in 326 B.C. A Moghul emperor, Jehangir (1605-1627) is reputed to have had more than one hundred thousand elephants. Elephants, then, played a major role in military campaigns for many hundreds of years. Only male elephants are used in fighting since female elephants tend to run away from male elephants in confrontations. But male elephants also have musk periods that make them unsuitable for fighting during those periods.

It is estimated that India has 50 percent of all the wild elephants and 20 percent of all the "captive" or domesticated elephants in Asia. The wild elephants are a continual problem since wild herds of them often trample on farms and have been known to kill Indian farmers and others. In an article "The Domesticated Asian Elephant in India," S.S. Bist (and others) writes:

> The Asian elephant (*Elephs maximus*) enjoys a special status in the country and the elephant symbolizes the Indian ethos. It has been very closely associated with the religion, myths, history and cultural heritage of India for centuries. Protecting and ensuring the survival of the elephant means much more to an Indian that protecting just another endangered species. Although the tiger has been designated as the national animal or India, for most Indians the elephant is the *de facto* national animal. It has been rightly said that one cannot imagine India with the elephant.

Rock paintings suggest that Indians domesticated the elephant some six thousand years ago and ancient literary texts such as the Rig Veda and the Upanishads contain references to elephants. Nowadays, there are no military uses for elephants but they are used for logging, tourism, and symbolic status displays of one kind or another.

**Figure 6.8**
**A Painting of an Elephant in Udaipur City Palace Museum**

Elephants also play an important part in the Hindu religion and one of the religion's most important and most popular gods, Ganesha, has the body of a pot-bellied human, though he has four arms, not two, and the head of an elephant with one tusk. He is often shown riding on a mouse or with a mouse as an attendant. Ganesha's role in the Hindu religion is complicated and some Hindus consider him to be the supreme god. He is the son of Shiva and Parvati and is associated with good luck, intelligence, and prosperity. Many Indians place an image of Ganesha on their homes as a means, they hope, of helping them become prosperous.

The symbolism of the elephant god Ganesha and the mouse is one more example of the kind of extremes of scale one finds in Indian culture. Thus, in Rajasthan you find gigantic forts and, at the same time, miniature paintings and in India you find extremes of poverty and great wealth, though India now has a middle class estimated at around three hundred million people. This matter of extremes of scale may be connected with India's royal heritage, but we also see these extremes if the symbology of Ganesha and the mouse, which suggests that Indian religions may be behind the extremes of scale one finds in Rajasthan and India, in general. In the United States, the myth is that elephants are afraid of mice. In India, the myth is that Ganesha rides on a mouse (an impossibility except in the symbolic imagination) or is served by one—thus here as elsewhere in India, opposites are joined together in curious ways.

A guide told me that all the mahouts in India are Muslims, because Hindus would not feel comfortable prodding elephants, due to the connection between the Hindu God Ganesha and elephants. In many countries we see the same kind of thing: people who cannot do some things because of some religious prohibition find members of other religious to do those things for them. So, when it comes to the Indian's beloved elephants, the Muslims play an all-important role in Indian culture.

In one of those curious moments of serendipity, I was working on this book when I heard a program on National Public Radio with Edward Luce, the *Financial Times* editor for Southeast Asia, who was stationed in Delhi for many years. He described a recent visit there. Luce is the author of *In Spite of the Gods: The Strange Rise of Modern India* and had been interviewed a number of times on National Public Radio in recent weeks. He was staying on this visit with the family of his wife, who is Indian, and they decided to take a drive somewhere. Luce commented on the enormous changes that have taken place in India in recent years—the subject of his book. He described how they got into their car and quickly found themselves in a terrible traffic jam.

**Figure 6.9**
**Tourists on an Elephant at Amber Fort in Jaipur**

He said he immediately assumed it was because of a sacred cow or a group of cows that were wandering around, oblivious to traffic the way cows in India are. The reason for this traffic jam, it turned out, was not cows but a huge elephant that parked itself in the middle of the road, a few blocks away from where Luce got stuck in traffic. The elephant refused to move—despite the pleadings of his mahout.

Eventually, the elephant did move, but this little incident shows the way large animals like cows and elephants play a role in modern India. In America, large animals are kept on farms or zoos, away from people and from their consciousness of these animals. That is not the case in

India, where these animals are part of the average Indian's everyday life experiences. The only time Americans see elephants is when they go to the zoo, and increasingly zoos are closing down their elephant viewing areas because it is not humane to keep elephants penned up the way they are in most zoos.

When I checked into its sales, Luce's book was number 310 on the Amazon.com popularity list, which means it was selling very well—reflecting America's interest in and fascination by modern Indian society and culture. India combines the third world and the first world, is full of promise and also held back by its caste system and by incredible corruption. India is seen by many Americans as a work in progress and how it will turn out is a subject of considerable interest.

### Camels in Rajasthan

A camel, as the saying goes, is a horse designed by a committee. When you travel in Rajasthan, especially in the Thar desert and cities near it, you see many camels. You see them patiently plodding along by the sides of roads, with carts attached to them or with gigantic bales of hay in huge bags, slung over their humps and hanging down on their sides. Because of the structure of the camel's face, they have an air of being snooty, with their noses up high looking down on everyone. Camels are also supposed to be rather nasty at times, spitting at people or trying to bite people riding them.

There are a number of different breeds of camels. The most common are the Bikerani, which is the breed that is used to pull carts and carry goods; the Jaiselmari, which are very fast riding camels; and the Kachchhil, which are stocky camels that produce a great deal of milk. Camel milk is supposed to have many therapeutic uses, but it is not popular with Rajasthanis because of its strong taste, even though there is a big milk shortage in Rajasthan and India. One-humped camels are the most commonly seen camel in Rajasthan, which has an estimated seven hundred thousand or 70 percent of all the camels in India. The number of camels in Rajasthan has been dropping rapidly, perhaps by fifty percent in the past decade, due in part to a decline in their grazing grounds.

Camels are used for a number of purposes, one of the most important of which involves transporting goods. A Rajasthani man with a camel and a cart can support his family. Camel milk, which is nutritious, can help feed poor families. Camels, it turns out, only need around two kilograms of feed to produce a liter of milk compared to nine kilograms of feed for a liter of milk from cows. In addition, camel wool can be used for making rugs and blankets. (Because camel wool fibre is very short, its wool has only limited uses.) Camel leather is used to make jootis, drum covers, and other leather products. Camel dung is also considered an excellent fertilizer, almost as good as goat and sheep dung and better than cow dung—and camel urine is also considered as a valuable fertilizer. Camel meat can be eaten, but it is not popular, and camel bones can be processed to make fertilizer, so the camel gives a great deal, both in life and in death.

There is a huge camel fair in Pushkar every year that attracts many Indians who are buying or selling camels and large numbers of foreign and domestic tourists, as well, though camels are always being bought and sold all over Rajasthan and in other states as well. It is only when you are riding a camel, glancing down at the ground from a very high perch that you realize how huge these animals are. They are also extremely uncomfortable to ride, since they bounce riders side to side and up and down at the same time while they are walking and rock them, rather violently, back and forth when getting up from their kneeling position or returning to it. A wit once wrote a poem about horses saying that they head any list of bad to get on and, he insisted, they are worse to bet on. That poet had never ridden a camel or bet on one.

**Figure 6.10
Camels in Camel Farm near Bikaner**

**Figure 6.11
The Jaiselmer Fort**

## The Jaisalmer Fort

The Jaisalmer Fort towers above the city of Jaisalmer—a gigantic edifice with ninety-nine huge bastions—and inspires awe and incredulity when you see it. The size of the fort is remarkable and, in addition, it is strikingly beautiful, constructed of light yellow sandstone that shimmers in the afternoon sun. The fort was built in 1156 by a Rajput ruler, Jaisala (for whom Jaisalmer is named) and added to, over the years, by different rulers. Unlike many other forts in Rajasthan, the Jaisalmer fort is inhabited. Around a quarter of the old city's population still lives within the fort's walls. There are around sixty thousand people who live in Jaisalmer.

The fort at Jaisalmer was often besieged. In the Insight Guides *Rajasthan* (1988), Uma Anad writes:

> According to the ballads, the first siege occur during the reign of Alla-ud-din-Khilji (1295 A.D.-1315 A.D.), provoked by a foolhardy raid on the royal baggage caravan. For seven long years, the besieging army tried to starve out the defenders. Finally, they breached the ramparts, and the Bhattis, facing certain defeat, proclaimed the terrible rite of *johar*. Once the women and children had perished by sword or fire, the men, clad in ceremonial saffron and opium-intoxicated, opening the gates and rushed out to meet a heroic death. (179)

There were other sacks of the fort at Jaisalmer over the years but eventually the rulers of Jaisalmer established relationships with the Mughal rules of the area. So tourists who visit the fort at Jaisalmer can, in a sense, participate in history by visiting the legendary fort.

The military architects who designed Jaisalmer were quite ingenious. The fort is guarded by huge gates with protruding metal ornaments that were put there to disturb elephants, whose trunks would be irritated if they tried to break the gates with their trunks. In addition, the path to the gate is winding so it would be very difficult to move vehicles quickly to get up enough speed to batter the doors down. And the fort is on top of an eighty meter high hill, which gave those in the fort a considerable military advantage in earlier times.

What is most interesting is the degree to which the fort has been turned into a gigantic tourist destination—with Jain temples, hotels, restaurants, massage parlors, Havelis (large homes, many of which are now hotels and bed and breakfasts), gift shops, and other shops that cater to tourists. Despite its commercialization, the fort has a great deal of charm and it is generally full of tourists wandering around its tiny streets, which are also inhabited by many cows and buffalo. The rest of the population of the city spills out down the hill, on which the fort stands. Jaisalmer can be considered as a kind of Disneyland, except that Jaisalmer is real, with a long history, but they both are bounded areas devoted to tourism. The fort is a UNESCO World Heritage site, but it is also on the UNESCO list of endangered sites, since the drainage problems in the fort are destroying it; already two of the bastions have crumbled.

In Jaisalmer, married couples often have a colorful mural, usually with an elephant and other decorations, painted on the walls of their houses informing everyone who can read the script the names of the people who got married, when they got married, and their castes. This might seem strange, but it is not that different, if you think about it, from the marriage and engagement notices you find in the Sunday *New York Times* which often have photos of the couples and information about their families and education, which serves the same function.

If you wander into the town, its shops are paradigmatic—very much like all the other shops you see in India, namely fabric stores, bakeries, restaurants, rug stores, clothing stores, tailors, barbers, and pharmacies. In an area about a mile from the main tourist gate to the fort there is a fruit and vegetable market. This is the "real" India, in a relatively affluent city, that contrasts with the touristic India found in the fort—a sanitized and Westernized version of Indian culture and society.

Many tourists visit the ancient Jain temples inside the fort. These Jain temples like most Jain temples are full of incredibly intricate carvings and a sanctuary with a sacred figure, and statues of something like fifty prophets, each in a separate cubicle, along the periphery of the temple. The detail in the carvings becomes overwhelming and in some parts of the temples difficult to see, because in some areas, the light is not very good.

Jaisalmer is, it turns out, only a few hundred miles from the border with Pakistan, so it is not unusual to hear jets screaming in the sky and to see endless columns of tanks rolling along the roads leading to and from Jaisalmer and also conducting maneuvers in the sandy desert on either side of the roads. So once again, more than a thousand years after Mughals sacked the fort in Jaisalmer, soldiers and pilots in Rajasthan find themselves in a tense and an uneasy relationship with Muslims, except that now both India and Pakistan have fighter planes and bombers with atomic bombs instead of elephants and spears.

## The "Incredible !ndia" Advertising Campaign

As India develops its tourism industry, it has begun doing more and more advertising to attract foreign tourists. The present campaign, "Incredible !ndia," with an exclamation mark instead of an "I" in "India," generally features beautiful Indian women in Saris or other costumes against dramatic backgrounds. One six-page spread in a magazine showed a woman, in a gorgeous red sari, lying on a bed of plants, her right arm bent behind her head as the gazed upwards into the sky, lost in thought. There is a red flower in her hair.

On the next page we find a paragraph that reads as follows:

> FRESH PLEASURES With its wealth of iconic monuments and sweeping vistas, India has long appealed to travelers seeking culture, natural beauty, and spirituality. Yet these days the subcontinent also entices visitors with more worldly pleasures. Treasure-filled bazaars and boutiques make the country a shopper's heaven, while mouth watering regional cuisines lures epicureans from around the globe. World-class golf and a hip nightlife add to India's allure, helping to reveal the modern side of this ancient land.

Below this passage we see a longshot of the Taj Mahal and a collection of colorful pottery in the foreground.

On the next page we see a highly stylized profile of a bejewelled woman with a nose ring who is standing in front of a photo of the Pushkar fair. Some of the copy on this page reads as follows:

> Come drench yourself in the days and moments that glorify harvestsseasons, triumphs, joys, sorrows, battles, Gods and kings. This is the land with 365 days of sound and 360 degrees of colour. Incredible !ndia.

The remainder of the pages deal with things one can buy in India, leisure activities (pubs, golf) and Indian food. On the last page of the six-page "special advertising section," there is an advertisement for a very upscale Tauk World Discovery tour of India, sold through American Express, at $7,690 per person for eighteen days and seventeen nights.

The Indian government also publishes a fifty-page booklet, *"Incredible !ndia:* 101 Things to Do" in India, covering such things as: 1: Pop a "Gogappa" in your mouth (pastry puffs with cilantro flavored water in them); 2: Get Indian in your attire; 3. Buy "healing gems" (buy nine gems); 4: Get a "gold facial: get a 22 carat gold facial;" 5: Join a cookery class; 6: Design your hands (get henna coloring drawn on them); 7: Play cricket in the park: 8: Get married Indian style; 9: Visit an Indian home; 10: Learn Yoga. Number 101 is Let your hair fly (go windsurfing).

The cover of this booklet has the following images: a religious icon, a photo of a snow-capped mountain peak, a Caucasian woman in a yoga position, a canoe on an idyllic beach, a red-turbaned man with a camel, and a tiger. All these images suggest the diversity of experiences one can have in India.

Like all advertising, this campaign is full of hyperbole. There is an emphasis of pleasures, of various kinds, as India is presented as a country with "sweeping vistas," mouth-watering foods, world-class golf courses, a "hip" nightlife, "treasure-filled" shops and, as might be expected, exotic and beautiful Indian women in saris and other costumes. India is portrayed as an incredible country that has many different regions with varied tourism possibilities in each. What the advertising doesn't tell you is what you sometimes find out when reading about in newspapers—the "con" sides of things, such as crowded roads and polluted beaches.

It is fair to say that there are two Indias: the India that most Indians experience and the "tourist" India that tourists experience—in their hotels that are generally somewhat separated from daily life in India. Tourists live in cocoons or "first world bubbles") of varying degrees of separation from everyday life in India. But, to be fair to India, tourists in most every country are removed from everyday life, no matter how hard they may try to escape from these bubbles. And in some cases, such as in India, it is very hard to escape from the hotel compounds in which first world travelers find themselves.

In an article in the *New York Times* titled "The Myth of the New India," Pankaj Mishra offers a different picture from the one given in the "Incredible !ndia" campaign. After commenting that the conventional business centric view of India suppresses a great deal of information, we read that (July 6, 2006, page A23):

> the country's $728 per capital gross domestic product is just slightly higher than that of sub-Saharan Africa.... It [India] ranks 127, just two rungs above Myanmar and more than 70 below Cuba and Mexico. Despite a recent reduction in poverty levels, nearly 380 million Indians still live on less than a dollar a day.... Despite the country's growing economy, 2.5 million Indian children die annually, accounting for one out of every five child deaths worldwide.... In the countryside, where 70 percent of India's population lives, the government has reported that about 100,000 farmers committed suicide between 1993 and 2003.

So there are some grim realities to be considered by tourists contemplating visits to India and many tourists are put off by the poverty there, even though most tourists who visit India generally have little direct contact with the desperately poor people there. For some travelers, just being in a country where there are so many poor people and so much suffering is enough to dissuade them from going to India.

## Indian Matrimonial Advertisements

It's fascinating to study the matrimonial pages of the *Sunday Times* and other newspapers in India. There are various categories of matrimonial such as: cosmopolitan, by community, by language, by profession, by religion, by caste and by region or state in India. Let me quote a few of the advertisements. I have written out all the abbreviated words for ease of reading, fixed grammatical errors, and deleted material of no interest. The BHP you see in the advertisements stands for: Biographical data, Horoscope, and Photograph.

\* \* \*

Kayastha Family Invites Tall, Fair, Handsome, Cultured & Athletic Built Engineer, M.B.A. Boy. Manager MNC Delhi Based

Highly Educated & Settled Family looking for Extremely Beautiful and Very Fair Bride. Decent Family. Send BHP...

\* \* \*

[Wanted] Slim Girl, Beautiful, Convent Educated B.D.S./

Professionally Qualified Girl from Status Mahur Family

For Very Handsome Smart, Fair Anshik Manglik Mahur Boy

29/175 Graduate Fully in Father's Surgical Equipments Business

Only Son Having Commercial Property in Central Delhi & other Places. Send your B/H/P...

# A Semiotic Perspective of Rajasthan (and the Golden Triangle) 75

\* \* \*

**Chattergee** Boy, 27/5'4" MBA Sales Executive in Reputed Co. 3LPA Seeks Fair, Beautiful, Convent Educated Girl. Send BHP...

\* \* \*

We must keep in mind that a very large percentage of marriages in India are arranged by the parents of the bride and groom, who, it must be surmised, keep in the mind the notion of marrying their sons and daughters to partners who are similar in caste, class, education and culture and who have a good chance of staying together.

There is a relatively small percentage of divorces in India because of the stigma connected with divorce and because so many women are completely dependent on their husbands, financially speaking. But as more women become educated and get good jobs, this situation is changing and so we find, if you look at the matrimonial pages, that a number of the people advertising have been divorced.

Many of the advertisements say that caste is no barrier but, for the most part, it is the fair (light-skinned), slim, beautiful, convent educated "girls" that all the fair, handsome "boys" with advanced degrees are looking for (and vice versa). They are unlikely to want Dalits (untouchables) and most will probably be in the caste of people in the business world. The use of the terms "boys" for men—all of whom are handsome—who are in their thirties and "girls"—all of whom are beautiful--who are in their twenties and thirties may also tell us something about Indian attitudes about the status of men and women who aren't married and don't have children.

In the United States, we have a number of sites on the Internet where people who are looking for husbands and brides find ways of finding one another, so we should not poke fun at these matrimonial advertisements, for many people in America and other countries do the same thing, though perhaps not with the same insistence on documented credentials and with less hyperbole. And now it is possible to respond to matrimonials in India by e-mail, so the Indians are moving into electronic means of searching for partners. As the *Times of India* box on one of the matrimonial ad pages dealing with e-mails puts it, "Now your life partner could be just a click away."

The fact that the advertisements ask for horoscopes suggests another dimension to the calculations men and women and their families take into consideration. It might seem strange that a family with a son who is a highly educated scientist or engineer would consider horoscope information, but we must remember we are dealing with a foreign culture with different perspectives on many areas of life. The divorce rate in the United States is approximately 50 percent and the rate in India is little over 1 percent, so one might surmise that using horoscope readings makes sense for Indians.

It is not the horoscope but the stigma connected with divorce and the problems women who are divorced face in getting remarried that are probably the main reasons so many Indian marriages don't end in divorce. As might be expected, the rate of divorce of Indian in cities is higher than in small villages, where the stigma is greatest and family influence is strongest.

One thing these matrimonial advertisements reflect is that even in a country with more than a billion people, where a large percentage of marriages are arranged, a goodly number of young men and women, and some who are not so young, still have trouble finding suitable partners.

### A Nation of Shopkeepers of Small Shops

India has the distinction of having the highest retail outlet density in the world, with more than five stores (though some sources say as many as eleven) per thousand people, according to various articles in newspapers and on the Internet. There is some disagreement between sources which suggest that there are either twelve million or fifteen million small retail stores in India, most of which are run by a single family. You see stores of all kinds, crammed next to one another, in seemingly endless profusion, when you walk around any city or town. Some of them are no larger than ten or fifteen feet wide—literally small holes in the wall.

Notes I kept in my journal from varying newspapers and magazines in India that I read when I was there offer more statistics on this matter of small stores in India:

Some 96 percent of stores in India are less than 500 square feet

There are eleven stores per thousand people in India

There are forty-five stores per thousand people in Delhi

There are four stores per thousand people in the United States

About 50 percent of Indians are self-employed

The image one gets from this article is of something vaguely resembling a beehive of very small shops in India. But things are changing.

January 30, 2007 marked the beginning of a new trend in the grocery business, with the opening of the first Reliance Fresh "Western-style" supermarket grocery stores in Delhi, a sprawling city of some fifteen million people. Reliance is rushing in to get established before Wal-Mart and other supermarket chains enter the country as wholesalers, since Indian law prevents foreign supermarkets for establishing themselves at the retail level. Reliance hopes to achieve twenty-five billion in sales by 2010 and hopes to have stores in 784 cities and 6,000 small towns. Reliance will also allow small groceries to purchase things from its stores at wholesale prices, so it won't completely devastate the small "mom and pop" stores.

This development shows how India is moving into the modern age in areas other than its advanced Internet technology sector and doing something to ease the growth of modern, Western-style supermarkets. But it would seem that the handwriting is on the wall for the small grocery stores. The average shopper in Reliance stores now spends around $3.40 per visit—which is a reflection of the fact that most (96 percent) Indians don't have refrigerators yet and that millions of others live just above the poverty level.

# Part 3

## Rajasthan Remembered

# 7

# Remembering Rajasthan

*Much of Rajasthan is arid. The Thar desert, comprising the northwestern third of the state, is a sparsely populated region with an austere climate that had dictated a limited menu. During times of famine, sustenance comes from the few deep-rooted plants that survive when all other vegetation has dried up. A dish made of three desert famine foods is kair sangria kumita. It has a small, berry-like fruit (kair) from a leafless thorny tree, a small bean pod (sangri) that grows on a different thorny tree and another desert berry (kumitra). This preparation is identified with the Marwari community.*

—Joan Peterson and Indu Menon, Eat Smart in India

*The stark, arid landscapes of the desert state have led to extraordinary forms of survival: enormous and imposing rock-hewn fortress-towns; ancient methods of water conservation; vibrantly coloured fabric worn by the local people to protect them from the sun; and a hot, spicy cuisine derived from meager resources. Boosted with limited fresh vegetables, fruits or fish, Rajasthani cuisine makes the best of cereals, pulses, spices and milk products to produce a cuisine that is surprisingly elaborate and reflects the lifestyle of the Rajputs (warrior clans) who originate here.*

—Martin Hughes with Sheema Mookherjee and Richard Delacy, World Food India

## Recollections of a Remarkable Tour

Let me take a moment to summarize some of the points I made earlier. I suggested that, generally speaking, there are three stages that tourists go through when they travel. The first involves the imagined trip, and since we are dealing with India, I call it "Imagined India." This is the stage when you imagine being in India and try to anticipate what travel there will be like. This is a form of research that tourists do so they will be informed about the place they are planning to visit. Before we went to India, I purchased half a dozen books on India and Indian history and culture and my wife read a gigantic novel, *A Suitable Boy,* by Vikram Seth and a number of other novels by Indian writers.

One article I read, in the March 2006 *National Geographic Traveler,* "I came in search of authentic India," by Rudy Maxa, dealt with, among other things, his visit to Jodhpur in Rajasthan. His description of the city of Jodhpur, which we were to visit on our tour of Rajasthan, was dramatic (March, 2006):

> The city's main streets resemble . . . the set of an Indiana Jones movie. Camels haul wooden carts piled high with cargo. Cows occupy traffic lanes, oblivious to vehicles that swerve to avoid them. Dogs roam everywhere. There are no sidewalks, just wide stretches of sand or dust with piles of rocks or refuse in front of one room storefronts selling car parts, packets of betel nuts, cell phones and clothing. Women in bright saris—crimson, saffron, and emerald—carry baskets of vegetables or stones on their heads or sweep the sand in front of their shops with brooms made of twigs. (99)

This is the India we see in videos and films, full of cars with their horns blaring, buses overflowing with passengers, and motorized rickshaws decorated with photographs of movie stars and rock musicians.

This passage is typical of the kind of descriptions you find in travel magazines and books about India and it gave me, in my mind's eye, an image of India that I was to find to be quite accurate. Jodhpur's skyline is dominated by a gigantic fort, the Meherangarth (majestic) fort—an edifice of truly astounding size. You can only imagine how many thousands of workers and elephants and how much money was spent in building the fort, which was started in the fifteenth century and added on to over the years as different rulers took control of it. Maxa's article dealt mostly with things to buy in Jodhpur, which wasn't of great interest to me, though shopping is an important element in tourism because people like to bring back souvenirs of their travels.

Whenever I tell anyone that I had traveled in India, they almost always make the same comment. "How did you cope with the poverty there?" People who have never been to India think it is full of beggars and impoverished people and that tourists in India find themselves besieged by them all the time. It is true that there are, unfortunately, hundreds of millions of poor and impoverished people in India but visitors to India do not find themselves surrounded by them whenever they leave their hotels or various tourist sites.

A good example of what I would suggest is a dated image of India comes from Miguel Serrano's book, *The Serpent of Paradise: The Story of an Indian Pilgrimage*. Serrano, who was Chile's ambassador in India for nine years, offers a terrifying picture of the poverty one finds in some places in India. He writes about Delhi as follows (1963):

> All along the street, beggars and sick and dying people wander into traffic, and what is seen daily in Old Delhi surpasses the imagination. Totally naked men and women, lying on the pavement and covered with flies and ants, are utterly ignored by the priests and rich merchants who pass by. Death and destruction everywhere evident. Men mutilated by syphilis or leprosy go along the sidewalks, stepping in their own

urine, and displaying their open red wounds. Some are deformed monsters, without faces or arms, and some have no legs. (21)

He adds that it is during the night when things are worst for Indians; and Indians, who don't seem to be humans, sit in their excrement and eat dead flesh. What is most remarkable, he says, is that ordinary people are indifferent to the misery they find all around them. They don't help the beggars, and the beggars who ask for alms never thank people for giving them money since they are doing people a favor for begging for money and allowing people, by giving alms, to improve their destinies.

Serrano's description of India is simply terrifying. We must keep in mind that his book was published in 1963, and there have been incredible changes in India since he wrote the book. And there is also the possibility that he exaggerated things. I would suggest that many people still think of India the way Serrano describes it, which means that those tourists who venture into India are not the ordinary tourists, but those with more of a sense of adventure and more willing to take risks than the typical tourist.

He made another comment about India that I found rather curious. He wrote, in his chapter "Meaningless Faces," that no buildings or paintings in India had generated any profound emotions in him. As he explained, everything he saw was "archetypal," and all the temples resembled one another and all the saintly men resembled all the other saintly men. (1963:135).

Serrano, I would suggest, was not a sympathetic observer of Indian life and culture, perhaps because he couldn't appreciate the symbology in these buildings and paintings. He does have a point, though, about the replication that takes place in many aspects of Indian culture—for many temples are like one another, many shops are like one another, and many villages are like one another as well.

The second stage involves actual travel in India, involves being there, and all the different experiences tourists have in the course of their travels. I have suggested that tourism can be thought of as, in essence, a semiotic enterprise that involves searching for significant sites to see and having enriching experiences of one kind or another. One reason people travel is that they are in search of experiences that they believe will enhance and enrich their lives and provide a number of different gratifications. I must confess that I found Jodhpur to be one of the least interesting cities we visited, though it certainly exhibited the chaos Rudy Maxa wrote about in his article on his visit to India and his search for the "authentic" India.

**Figure 7.1
Puppeteer at Work**

Tourists are always searching for authenticity but, in many cases, what they find is some ersatz version of the culture that people in the country think is best designed for foreign visitors. Thus, "fake" Indian food might seem more Indian to tourists than real Indian food, and some dances are doctored to suit the tastes of foreigners. One of the dilemmas tourists face is that they want to find wonderful places to visit but don't like to find hordes of other tourists in those places. The secret is to find places before they are discovered, but in this age, as soon as any place is discovered, it soon fills up with tourists. That is what is happening in Rajasthan and all through India now that it is "hot."

The third stage involves remembering one's trip. As I explained earlier, tourists often keep journals, take many photographs, and purchase souvenirs from the places they visit. And now, with digital cameras being so popular, many tourists download their cameras onto their computers and arrange to have these photos appear as slideshows when they pause for a certain amount of time while typing. They often put these photographs in large books that they can look at to remember their trips—places they saw, people they met, things they did. It is also possible to buy electronic frames that display images from the cards used to store photos in cameras, so you can have digital photos appearing in slideshows all the time to remind you of your trips.

In this final section of the book, I will deal with some of my experiences in Rajasthan and the Golden Triangle that may help illuminate what traveling in Rajasthan is like. I offer a commentary on my experiences in Rajasthan and hope that, while my narrative is personal, it may provide some insights into various aspects of Indian culture and provide an idea of what travel in Rajasthan and India is like. In many cases, the full impact of our travel doesn't strike us until we've returned home and start remembering the experiences we've had. The more I think about my stay in India, the more I realize how remarkable it was—for India was an experience unlike any other travels I've had, and, I would say, most people who have traveled in India would say the same thing.

### The Airport in Delhi

The airport in Delhi provides many international tourists with their first experience of India. When we deplaned in Delhi, we found ourselves, after a short walk, in a very large and rather dingy room where people waited in long lines to have their passports stamped by immigration officials so they could then go through customs. There must have been ten or more immigration workers in booths, who processed the tourists as quickly as they could, but it took a good twenty or thirty minutes for us to get to an immigration officer. We had no trouble getting through the process, but the rundown nature of the room we all waited in foreshadowed what we would encounter—for an overwhelming proportion of the buildings in India seem to be in a state of disrepair and deterioration.

As I waited in line, I glanced around the room. "It could use a good coat of paint," I thought. I'm not sure whether the reception room at the airport is a good way to introduce tourists to India—in that it provides them with an accurate picture of what much of India is like—or if it is a bad idea—in that it provides a rather negative first impression. After we cleared customs we walked out of the airport and found ourselves in a passageway lined on both sides by drivers and others holding slips of paper or cardboard with the names of people they were sent to meet. There were hundreds of them and as we walked down the passageway and looked for our name, we wondered whether someone would actually be there to meet us.

When you travel to distant lands, you always have a slight tinge of anxiety wondering whether everything is going to work out the way you hope it will. "What will we do if our driver isn't there?" I wondered. Fortunately, our driver, Roshan had been sent to meet us. We were to spend the next twenty-four days with him and learn a great deal about his village and his wife and even more about his father.

In reading comments on the Internet about Indira Gandhi International Airport, as it is now called, I noticed that numbers of the people writing were amazed that the capital of a powerful country like India would have an airport in its capitol city like it. Others complained about the huge waiting room, where you have to wait before you can go through security checks, and the general lack of facilities in the airport. When we were returning to America, we had to wait for a few hours in that waiting room, which has very few chairs. When we finally got into the area where we were waiting for our flight, there was more seating but hardly any restaurants. I ended up getting a six-inch sandwich at a Subway restaurant that is located at one end of the large pre-boarding room.

Our flight from Delhi took us to Singapore, where we also had to wait, but the airport in Singapore is new and is very modern and posh—one of the great international airports and the equal of airports in Hong Kong, some airports in the United States, and those found in many European countries. The Singapore airport is also reflective of the country, which seems to have created itself out of almost nothing in the past few decades. India, on the other hand, is ancient and so is the airport in Delhi. The "new" terminal was built in 1986. The airport was designed to handle 12 million passengers and it handles around 16 million passengers. So the message of the airport is that it has been asked to do more than it should be doing. We see this in other areas in India—in the roads and trains and many other aspects of life there. You see this when you travel by car and come upon enormous lines of huge Tata trucks rolling along or parked and waiting for the time when they will be allowed in cities. They are generally decorated with paintings and have "please use horn to pass" painted on their backs.

There are plans for a new terminal at the airport; in the not too distant future, Delhi should have a terminal that reflects its status. The rest of India is racing to create a new, more modern India—the India you see in the ultra-modern call-center buildings and high-tech campuses that you see here and there in India. There are gigantic road building projects going on in India as it works to solve its infrastructure problems, so it can accommodate more tourists and facilitate the movement of goods from one place to another.

## Pigs Eat Three-Year-Old Boy

The first day we were in India, November 29th, 2006, a newspaper was delivered to our room and it had an incredible story in it. It seems that a three-year-old boy had wandered away from his family while they were having a meal and was attacked and eaten by a herd of pigs. I was shocked and couldn't help but wonder what our tour of India, which was just about to start, would be like. India, I thought, is a country of unspeakable horrors and incredible wonders. That seems to be one of the most important insights I had about India—that it is a country of extremes of all kinds—where artists paint incredibly detailed miniature paintings and maharajahs build forts of gigantic size, where some people are incredibly wealthy (India has more than thirty billionaires now) and hundreds of millions of people are very poor, where there are a million engineers who graduate every year, but only 4 percent of the population has refrigerators. India is a gigantic puzzlement. It is not a country where moderation rules and its history reflects that fact.

India, it occurred to me, doesn't seem to be a country as much as a parallel universe, existing and carrying on in its own way with its old ways as it absorbs the forces of modernization. Some of the statistics on India are simply incredible—more than a billion people, fifty million pilgrims bath themselves in a ritual ceremony in the Ganges, there are hundreds of languages and numerous dialects and scripts, and mind-boggling statistics about all kind of other things.

I was a tourist and so only exposed, in chance encounters that took place occasionally and by accident, to the "real" India—the India in which there are an estimated three hundred million middle-class people (some estimates put the figure at only fifty million), who live, more or less, the way we do in the first world. I took a walk outside of my hotel in Bikaner, the Karni Bhawan, which was located on the outskirts of the city. It was an old art deco hotel—a remarkably incongruous structure that only had ten rooms. Our room was the largest hotel room I've even been in and was, in truth, the size of a suite of rooms. There was a housing development of really handsome homes, as nice as any middle-class homes you might find anywhere in the United States, located across the street from it. And in a field in between two of them, there was an encampment of gypsies living in a tent. So in that walk I found two extremes and that seems to me to characterize the country.

So there are hundred of millions of middle-class Indians and eight hundred million Indians who live in poverty or just on the edge of poverty. India is a country in which thousands of poor farmers commit suicide every year because their situation is so utterly hopeless. And yet, you also feel, as you ride by all those very modern call centers scattered here and there in India, that India is on the move. Everything you read in the newspapers suggests that in a few years India will have a larger economy than that of Great Britain and other Western European countries and will be an economic giant.

India has the highest percentage of shops to people in the world, but it is soon to have a number of huge supermarkets. This means that the whole system of purchasing food will eventually change, though since so only a small percentage of people have refrigerators, the Indians won't be shopping the way people in America do for quite a while. So what is the "real" India? I hoped I would gain some insights into India by doing a thorough tour of Rajasthan.

## The Camel Ride in the Thar Desert Near Jaisalmer

On our tour of Rajasthan from Jasbhag Tours, the prospectus said something to this effect: "And now, for the highlight of your trip, a camel safari in the Thar Desert." There was something rather wonderful about driving through the Thar Desert, located between the various cities we visited. The sun was always shining and the sky was always a brilliant blue color. For long periods of time we would be the only car on the road and the desert seemed empty of any life, and then, every once in a while, you'd see a woman in a brilliantly colored sari, walking by the side of the road or come to a small village with just a few houses.

We arrived in Jaisalmer, after a long drive, and spent the night at the Rang Mahal hotel, a very modern hotel built to resemble an ancient fort with beautiful grounds and a gigantic swimming pool. We drove by the Jaisalmer Fort, which was strikingly perched on the top of a hill and shining brilliantly in the sun. The next morning our driver brought us to "Resort Rawla," a large encampment in the desert about thirty kilometers from Jaisalmer. Jaisalmer is an important tourist destination, thanks to its fantastic fort and the possibility of taking camel rides in the desert. There were more than a dozen thatched huts and a similar number of tents at the resort. Some of the tents were more expensive than the huts because these tents had bathrooms (in cement block rooms) with running water, attached to them. There was no electricity—the lights were all solar powered. We stayed in one of the tents with a bathroom.

After we settled into our tent, it was time to go on the camel safari. One of the employees of the resort asked us, "Do you want the two hour ride or the three hour ride?" We walked over to an area where the camel owner and some other people were chatting. The camel, Rajah, was sitting on the ground. A number of people were gathered around him, chatting with the camel driver. Getting on the camel was easy while it was sitting on the ground, but when the camel got up, first we were pushed backwards and then forwards; and when he stood up, we found that we were quite high above the ground. We ended up settling for the half hour ride, terrified all the time that we'd fall off Rajah.

When the sun was out, the desert was warm and very pleasant. The man who owned the camel, a young man, walked very slowly and kept saying, "careful Rajah, careful." He guided Rajah, over some very flat parts of the desert for about a half hour and then had Rajah sit so we could get off. Getting off turned out to be difficult for me as I was wedged in behind my wife, so the camel owner had to grab me and pull me off Rajah. Later, we watched the sun set in the desert—it was a beautiful moment. We watched from the top of a sand dune about a ten minutes walk away from the resort. We could see tents from another resort in the distance and hear some goats that were wandering around a few hundred yards from us.

That night, the resort brought in a gypsy dancer and some wonderful musicians to entertain us while we had dinner in a yard by the dining hall. They played with enormous passion and spirit. There were five other guests at the resort (from Portugal, I discovered) who averted their eyes when we walked by and pretended we didn't exist. I found their behavior quite bizarre. It started getting cold during the dancing and music performance so we all went into the dining hall where the musicians and dancers set up and continued to entertain us.

After dinner, which consisted of a number of Rajasthani dishes, we went back to our tent and went to bed. We wore our clothes and fleece jackets and piled our blankets on top of ourselves. I can't recall ever being so cold. I can remember thinking, "It seems crazy that I paid money to suffer like this." My wife slept through the night but I got up in the

**Figure 7.2**
**Tourists on a Camel in Thar Desert**

middle of the night and wandered around the compound for a half an hour. The next morning we had breakfast and our driver brought us back to our hotel in Jaisalmer where we took showers and prepared to go off on our own visit to the town. We had a simple lunch in a little restaurant in Jaisalmer.

There are camels in Rajasthan because much of it is a desert—mostly scrub, with little bushes growing here and there. Our camel driver, who told us he only had a fourth grade education but who spoke English perfectly, told us that they haven't always had camels in Rajasthan—only for a few hundred years or so. The camels and the small donkeys that are found in Rajasthan made me think of our trip in Morocco, where these animals are also found in great numbers.

During our tour, we went to a camel farm where hundreds of camels were being held in large, fenced-off areas, eating and wandering around.

**Figure 7.3**
**Musicians at Resort Rawla in the Thar Desert**

A keeper, who wanted them to move to a different field, opened the gate then took out a handkerchief and started waving it around. The camels got excited and raced out of the pen in great haste. I found it curious that these huge animals could be controlled so easily. There were groups of tourists from different countries wandering around the camel farm, taking photographs of the camels. Most people don't associate India with camels, but with tigers and elephants. But in a desert state like Rajasthan, there are many camels.

## Dining in Rajasthan

Rajasthani food is often described as spicy—an adjective that doesn't really do justice to the food we had during our tour of Rajasthan and the Golden Triangle. Rajasthani food is a regional variation of Indian food, just as southern food in America is a regional variation of American cuisine. Even though we always asked our waiters to have the cooks "tone down" the spicy quality of the food, most of the time what we received ranged from mildly spicy to very hot. This often led to our occasionally ordering either Chinese or Continental dishes from the menus at the hotels where we dined when there wasn't a buffet. All the hotels we stayed at also had Chinese and Continental/Western food on their menus.

Hotels and restaurants with buffets often serve Western foods as well as Rajasthani/Indian ones. In one of our hotels, the buffet had roast chicken, roast potatoes, and other Western foods—all of which were beautifully cooked. Breakfasts in hotels, with rare exceptions, are buffets and have Western foods as well as Indian foods. Typically, these buffets generally have juice, sliced papaya, cold and hot cereals, milk, tea, coffee, toast, fried eggs, and omelets (generally prepared to order by a cook) as well as Indian food for Indian guests.

At one hotel we stayed at, the Castle Mandawa, the food was very refined and the dining experience was quite remarkable. There were perhaps ten tables located around the perimeter of a square open-air area. We dined beneath the stars. In the middle of the room, there was a large bonfire. Waiters brought us soup, a salad, and then placed eight different foods on our dinner plates. The service was very discreet and I noticed that the maitre d' was wearing jodhpurs and shiny black leather boots. Then we were entertained by two different troupes of dancers. In one, an elderly man did a fire dance, leading a parade of musicians. He started on a balcony, overlooking the open-air dining room and then came down some stairs and danced before each table. Shortly after that, a troupe with a mother, a father (playing musical instruments), and two children dancers came and entertained the guests, also stopping before each table. It was a magical evening.

One of the biggest anxieties many tourists have in coming to India involves the food there and the fear they have of getting sick. I must confess that I did get sick for one day. We were in between hotels and stopped at a very elegant restaurant. It also had an open courtyard but our waiter seated us inside because all the tables in the courtyard were reserved for French tourists who soon poured into the restaurant and filled all the tables there. My wife and I split a thali, which is a series of different Indian dishes, all in little bowls. The thali had too much food for one person, I should add. Because she cannot eat yoghurt, I ate the yoghurt and believe I got sick from it. Aside from that, I had no problems and felt secure in eating salads, fruit, and any other foods on the menus.

Tourists who dine in good hotels and tourist restaurants, I would say, need not fear eating anything. Except for my upset stomach that lasted one day, my wife and I ate anything we wanted to eat with no problems. Often we ate a mixture of Indian foods and Continental foods, selecting Indian foods that seemed unlikely to be too spicy.

In the guidebooks one will read that one shouldn't eat any fruit unless it can be peeled and avoid foods that are found in buffets. It is always

**Figure 7.4
The Castle Mandawa Hotel in Mandawa**

possible that tourists will get sick from eating Indian food in good restaurants and in hotels, but based on spending almost a month in Rajasthan, I would say that the fears tourists have about food in India are for the most part unfounded—providing, of course, that they avoid street food. We dined in some humble restaurants that we found while wandering around and never had any trouble.

In looking over the reports on India in Frommer's "Travel Talk," I came across any number of comments about how disinterested and uncooperative clerks and waiters in Indian hotels are, but I found just the opposite to be the case. My wife was coming down with a cold when we were in Jaisalmer, and when we went to dinner our first night in the Rang Mahal's large and beautiful dining room, after the Maitre d' seated us, I asked for some tea for my wife. He said "My name is Khet." He ordered one of his waiters to bring us a pot of tea, some milk, and then Khet brought us two bowls of delicious chicken soup. He also made sure we tried various dishes at the buffet, spooning off sauces that he thought were too spicy for us. On our second and last night, he ordered dishes that weren't on the menu for us.

Our two dinners at the hotel were really quite wonderful. We were so surprised and delighted by the care we received that we arranged to have one of the clerks take a photo of the three of us in the lobby. I would estimate Khet was in his early fifties. When we thanked him for being so attentive, he said "You remind me of my parents." In India, where parents play such a major role in their lives of their children, I'd like to think that it was quite a compliment and not a comment on my having reached my "golden years."

Curiously, in a few of the hotels we stayed at, we were the only people in the dining room or there were only two or three couples in them. In these cases, since there were so few people, the hotels didn't make a buffet and we ordered from the menu. And in some restaurants, even though there were many people in the restaurant, there wasn't a buffet. We stayed in the Connaught Hotel in Delhi for two nights in a modest and not very pleasant room. But the restaurant in the Connaught was quite wonderful. The service was exceptional and the food was delicious.

In addition, there were musicians there who were brought in to entertain us. The first night, they came in, set up, and then sat around a table drinking. I asked the Maitre d' when they were going to play.

"Around 9:00 PM," he said.

"Too bad," I replied, "because I would like to have heard them."

The restaurant opened at 7:30 and a number of people came in at that time to eat. The next evening I noticed that the musicians started playing a bit after 7:30 PM. I guess it had not dawned on the people who ran the restaurant that the musicians should play when the restaurant opened and they should not wait around until 9:00 PM. The musicians, I should add, had a bored look on their faces.

Our waiter at the Connaught asked me, "Do you like India?"

"Very much," I said. "It's a wonderful country."

He smiled, full of pride.

### Roshan and the Cell Phone

Most of our trip was in Rajasthan, and while he was driving us from city to city, our driver, Roshan, was constantly answering calls on the cell phone he was using—paid for by Amandeep Singh, the owner of Jasbhag Tours. Many of the calls were from Amandeep, who was calling to find out how things were going. After each call, he would tell us who called. He'd say "that was from my boss," or "that was from my wife," or "that was from my cousin." He generally showed no emotion during the calls and, since he spoke in Rajasthani or Hindi, I had no idea of what he was talking about in his conversations. Often, the calls related to family matters.

During one call, I noticed that Roshan was very assertive, almost shouting. His voice was unusually loud. After the call ended, he explained, "That was from my tenant. He's late in paying the rent. I get a thousand rupees a month rent from him for a house I own."

So every day, the calls came in. And Roshan probably made some other calls during the hours when he was on his own, staying at the little guest houses where drivers stay when they aren't ferrying tourists around. But at soon as we passed from Rajasthan into Uttar Pradesh, he put the phone away.

"There are roaming charges in Uttar Pradesh," he said, "so I turned off the cell phone. I only turn it on when I have to call my boss."

The statistics on cell phone use in India are quite remarkable. Around 15 percent of Indians have cell phones, but its use is growing by an estimated 6.5 million new subscribers a month. It is anticipated that by 2010 there will be around 400 million cell phone users in India, which will mean approximately 30 percent of Indians will have cell phones. In the United States, more than 70 percent of the people have cell phones, but we lag far behind some countries in Europe which have 100 percent saturation. Some countries, it turns out, have more cell phones than people in them. The impact of these cell phones on Indian culture will be remarkable, because cell phones, we now know, play an important role in the countries where they are found and have a profound social and political impact.

### The Pushkar Girl

Once we had our travel plans made, I started reading the postings on the Frommer's "Travel Talk" website for India. There are sites for most countries on that website. You can get a sense of how popular countries are by looking at the number of postings for each country. Albania has hardly any postings and Greece has more than a thousand.

I knew we would be staying in a hotel in the Connaught circle area and so I posted a question asking for suggestions for good restaurants in that area. I received a number of replies. There are some people who seem to spend their lives on the India site answering questions posted by people. One person who sent me an answer used the name "Pushkar Girl," which made me assume that she was an Indian woman living in Pushkar, where the huge camel fair is held every year.

I thanked her for her comments and asked her another question, which she answered. We traded messages, all posted on the "Travel Talk" website, and then one day she suggested we bypass the Frommer website and send messages to one another by e-mail. So I gave her my e-mail address and she sent me her address. After we sent a few messages, I wrote, "I live in a little town near San Francisco, since I used to teach at San Francisco State University." To my great surprise she wrote, "I also live in a little town near San Francisco." She sent me her telephone number. I had assumed she was an Indian woman living in Pushkar, but it turned out I was wrong. Then I thought she was an Indian woman living near San Francisco. And I was wrong again.

I wrote back. "I live in a little town called Mill Valley." She then wrote, "I also live in Mill Valley." So I called her and my wife and I invited her over for tea. She came, bringing, as gifts, maps of various cities in India and a lovely cloth bag. It turns out she's a Caucasian American women, and a girl only in the sense that a woman of fifty-ish and who is not married might be called a girl in Indian marriage advertisements. She loves Pushkar and has many friends there, so she goes there every year for the fair—hence "Pushkar Girl." Incidentally, my moniker on the Frommer's website is "Decoder Man," and that's because decoding cultures is one of the things I spend much of my time doing.

The Pushkar girl then sent us several messages inviting us over for tea. "Don't worry," she wrote in one of her e-mail messages, "I've not forgotten about you," but she never came up with a date and I think her mind may be occupied now with getting ready for the next Pushkar fair. It is now more than a year since we've heard from her and I suspect we will never get that invitation for tea.

## India in the News

One of the most remarkable things I noticed after I returned from India was that just about every day, for weeks on end, I've read something—sometimes two or three articles in one publication—about India in the various publications to which I subscribe. I should point out that I subscribe to the *New York Times,* the *San Francisco Chronicle,* the *Marin Independent-Journal,* the *Wall Street Journal,* the *Economist, Time Magazine, US News & World Report, Travel & Leisure,* and *Fortune,* so there's plenty of opportunity to find something on almost any subject in one of those publications.

Still, it is remarkable how much interest there is in India in the press. Some of this interest was due to takeovers by Indian companies or takeovers of Indian companies, but there was also a good deal of material about other aspects of Indian society and culture, such as India's prowess in graduating a million engineers each year, the various call centers and computer technology campuses found in India, and profiles of Indian businessmen who are assuming a more important role in the global economy. All these articles should stimulate interest by tourists in India and it is reasonable to suggest that large numbers of people will move from reading about India to wanting to go there and then to visiting the country. And there is much about tourism in India in the news and on radio and television, as well.

I hope that my book will help those interested in Indian culture obtain a better understanding of how the tourism industry in Rajasthan and India have been developing and what travel in Rajasthan and India is like. I also have provided some insights into Indian culture and society, in general. India is a remarkable country, with much to see in its many states, and if this book plays a role in enhancing the experiences that tourists have in Rajasthan and India, I feel my efforts on behalf of better understanding this wonderful country were not in vain.

# Bibliography

Anad, Uma, "Jaisalmer; Desert Citadel," in Insight Guides, *Rajasthan.* 1988. Singapore: APA Press
Barnouw, Victor. (1973). *Culture and Personality.* Homewood, IL: The Dorsey Press.
Berger, Arthur Asa. (2004). *Deconstructing Travel: Cultural Perspectives on Tourism.* Walnut Creek, CA: AltaMira Press.
Berger, Arthur Asa. (2000). *Media and Communication Research Methods.* Thousand Oaks, CA: Sage.
Bist, S.S. et al. "The Domesticated Elephant in India." http://www.fao.org/docrep/005/ad031e/ad031e0g.htm.
Cohen, Erik. (1972) "Towards a Sociology of International Tourism," *Social Research:* 35, No. 1, pp. 164-183.
Douglas, Mary. (1975). *Implicit Meanings: Essays in Anthropology.* London: Routledge & Kegan Paul.
Douglas, Mary and Aaron Wildavsky. (1982). *Risk and Culture: An Essay on the Selection of Technological and Environmental Dangers.* Berkeley, CA: University of California Press.
Douglas, Mary. "In Defence of Shopping." In Pasi Falk and Colin Campbell, eds. *The Shopping Experience.* (1997). London: Sage Publications.
Douglas, William O. (1951). *Strange Lands and Friendly People.* New York: Harper & Brothers.
Eames, Andres (ed.). (1997). *Insight Guides: India.* Singapore: APA Publications.
Forster, E.M. (1924). *A Passage to India.* New York: Harcourt, Brace and Company.
Grewal, Royina. (1997). *In Rajasthan.* Melbourne: Lonely Planet Journeys.
Harris, Marvin. (1974). *Cows, Pigs, Wars and Witches: The Riddles of Culture.* New York: Vintage Books.
Hughes, Martin with Sheema Mookherjee and Richard Delacy. (2001). *World Food India.* Victoria: Lonely Planet.
DK Travel Writers. (2002). *India.* London: DK Publishing
India Dairy Industry, "The Sacred Cow." http://www.indiadairy.com/info_sacred_cow.html.
"India Overheats," Feb. 3-9, page 11, 2007. *The Economist.*
Israel, Samuel and Toby Sinclair (eds.). (1988). *Insight Guides: Rajasthan.* Singapore: APA Publications.

Johnston, Harry. (no date given) *Pioneers in India.* London: Blackie and Son.
Kishore, Prem and Anuradha Kishore Ganpati. (2003). *India: An Illustrated History.* New York: Hippocrene Books, Inc.
Kolanad, Gitonjali. (2005). *Culture Shock: India,* Singapore: Marshall Cavendish Publications.
Lounsbury, B. (ed). (2003) *Let's Go India & Nepal.* New York: St. Martin's Press.
Luce, Edward. (2007). *In Spite of the Gods: The Strange Rise of Modern India.* New York: Doubleday.
MacCannell, Dean. (1976). *The Tourist: A New Theory of the Leisure Class.* New York: Schocken.
Masters, John. (1956). *Bugles and a Tiger: A Personal Adventure.* New York: Viking Press.
Maxa, Rudy. "I Came in Search of Authentic India." *National Geographic Traveler.* March, 2006: 94-104,
Mishra, Pankaj. "The Myth of the New India." *The New York Times.* July 6, 2006: A23.
Morris, Jan. (1982). *Destinations: Essays from* Rolling Stone. New York: Galaxy Books.
Navarane, V.S. "The Religions of India," in Andrew Eames, (ed.) *Insight Guide to India.* (1997). Boston: Houghton Mifflin.
Nehru, Jawaharlal. (1946). *The Discovery of India.* New Delhi: Oxford University Press.
Peterson, Joan and Indu Menon. (2004). *Eat Smart in India.* Madison, WI: Ginkgo Press.
Plog, Stanley. "Why Destinations Rise and Fall in Popularity." *Cornell Hotel and Restaurant Quarterly,* 14, No. 4: 55-59
"Sacred Cow." [http:www.indiadairy.com/info_sacred_cow.html.]
Serrano, Miguel. Transl. Frank MacShane. (1963). *The Serpent of Paradise: The Story of an Indian Pilgrimage.* London: Routledge & Kegan Paul.
Singh, Sarina et al. (2005).*India.* Tenth Edition. Lonely Planet Publications: Victoria.
Thompson, Michael, Richard Ellis and Aaron Wildavsky. (1990). *Cultural Theory.* Boulder, CO: Westview Press.
Van den Berghe, Pierre L. (1975). *Man in Society: A Biosocial View.* New York: Elsevier.
Wildavsky, Aaron. "Conditions for a Pluralist Democracy, or, Cultural Pluralism means More than One Political Culture" (Quoted in Berger, 1982:7)
Zeman, J. Jay. "Peirce's Theory of Signs" in T. Sebeok, *A Perfusion of Signs.* Bloomington: Indiana University Press.

# Index

Alexander the Great, 64
Anad, Uma, 70
Aurangzeb, 52

Barthes, Roland, 43
Berghe, Pierre L. van den, 27
Bikaner, 87
Bist, S.S., 66
Bombay, 47

Calcutta, 47
Castle Mandawa hotel, 92
Cohen, Erik:
 drifters, 23
 explorers, 23
 individual mass tourists, 23
 on "tourist bubble," 34
 organized mass tourists, 23
 typology of kinds of tourists, 34
"Conditions for a Pluralist Democracy, or, Cultural Pluralism means More than One Political Culture," 32
Connaught Hotel, 94
*Cornell Hotel and Restaurant Administration Quarterly*, 23
*Course in General Linguistics*, 42
*Cows, Pigs, Wars and Witches: The Riddles of Culture*, 62-64
*Cultural Theory*, 32-33
*Culture and Personality*, 17

*Deconstructing Travel: Cultural Perspective on Tourism*, 10
Delacy, Richard, 81
Delhi, 47, 86-87
*Destinations*, 47
Disneyland, 71
Djoser tours, 25

"Domesticated Elephant in India," 65
Douglas, Mary:
 Grid-Group tourism in India, 31-37;
 "In Defence of Shopping," 33-34, 36-37
Douglas, William O., 60-64
Dumont, Louis, 28

Eames, Andrew, 48
*Eat Smart in India*, 81
*Economist* magazine, 58-60, 96
Egypt, 11
Ellis, Richard, 32-33
Emerson, Ralph Waldo:
 "America, My Country," 27-28
*Empire of Signs*, 43
Exotic and everyday contrasted, 20

*Financial Times*, 66
*Fortune*, 96
Forster, E.M., 60
Frommer's "Travel Talk," 44

Golden Triangle, 5, 9
Gratifications of tourism, 18-23:
 curiosity about India satisfied, 20
 experiencing extreme empathy, 21-22
 experiencing the ugly, 21
 getting in touch with the beautiful, 21
 India is exotic, 19-20
Grid-Group Theory:
 and tourism typologies, 36
 lifestyles and, 32, 33
 tourism in India, 31-37
Grewal, Royina, 57
Gujarat, 9

*Homo Hierarchus*, 28
Hughes, Martin, 81

*Implicit Meanings*, 28-29
Incredible !ndia:
   advertising campaign, 72-74
   101 Things to Do booklet, 73
"In Defence of Shopping," 33-34
India:
   airport in Delhi, 85-86
   as parallel universe, 87
   growth of cell phone use, 95
   images of in *Economist* magazine, 58-60
   matrimonial advertisements, 74-76
   number of size of shops, 76-77
   reliance fresh supermarkets, 77
   sacred cows, 60-64
   small percentage of divorces, 75
India flag:
   religious divide, 47
   significance of colors in, 47
Indian Dairy Industry website, 62
India:
   anxieties felt by tourists planning visits, 12-13
   contrasted with America, 27-30
   country of origin of foreign tourists, 5-6
   foreign tourism in, 3-5
   hierarchical society, 27-30
   Hindu caste system, 29
   Hinduism and Islam polarities, 48-49
   image on Frommer's "Travel Talk," 10-11
   impact of globalization and new technologies, 30
   polar opposite of America, 30
   TripAdvisor postings on Indian hotels, 11-12
Indira Gandhi International Airport, 86
*In Rajasthan*, 57
Insight Guides *India*, 53
Insight Guides *Rajasthan*, 70-72
*Insight Guide to India*, 48
*In Spite of the Gods: The Strange Rise of Modern India*, 66
Intrepid tours, 25

Jahan, Shah, 52
Jaipur, 5
Jaisalmer, 70; fort, 88
Japan:
   semiotic analysis of, 43
Jehangir, 64

Karni Bhawan hotel, 87
Karni Mata, 55-57; Karni Mata temple, 55-57
Kolkatta (Calcutta), 59

*Let's Go India & Nepal*, 14, 18
Lévi-Strauss, Claude, 9
*Lonely Planet India*, 3, 36, 53
Luce, Edward, 66-68

MacCannell, Dean, 41
*Man in Society: A Biosocial View*, 27
*Marin Independent-Journal*, 96
Maxa, Rudy, 81-82
Mill Valley, California, 96
Mishra, Panjaj, 72-73
Mookherjee, Sheema, 81
Morocco, 11, 90
Morris, Jan, 47
Mustaches in Rajasthan, 54-55
"Myth of the New India," 73

*National Geographic Traveler*, 44, 81-82
National Public Radio, 66
Neoncarrot.com website, 5
New Delhi, 5
*New York Times*, 71, 73, 96

Palace of Winds (Hawa Mahal), 52-54
Panjaj Mishra, 72-73
Peirce, Charles Sanders, 42-43
"Peirce's Theory of Signs," 42
*Passage to India*, 60
*Perfusion of Signs*, 42
Plog typology:
   allocentrics, 23-24
   psychocentrics, 23-24
   travel to India and, 26
Pushkar Girl, 95-96

Rajasthan:
  camels, 68-69
  camel rides in, 88-90
  elephants and, 64-68
  food in, 91-94
  Jaiselmer Fort, 77-72
  Pushkar fair, 69
  titles of typical tours, 17
  typical itineraries, 18-19
Rang Mahal hotel, 88
Rathanbore National Park:
  importance of tigers, 57-58
  significance of term "safari," 58
Rat Temple at Deshnok, 55-57
Roshan:
  cell phone, 95
  driver, 94-95

Saussure, Ferdinande de, 42
Sawai Pratep Singh, Maharajah, 53, 54
*San Francisco Chronicle,* 96
San Francisco State University, 96
Sebeok, T., 42
Semiology, 42
Semiotics:
  perspective on Rajasthan and Golden Triangle, 47-77
  tourist imagination and, 43-45
Semiotic theory:
  Icons, 42
  Indexes, 42
  signified (concept), 42
  signifier (sound-object), 42
  symbols, 42
*Serpent of Paradise: The Story of an Indian Pilgrimage,* 82-83
Serrano, Miguel, 82-83
Sesser, Stan, 9
Seth, Vikram, 81
Shah Jahan, 52
Singh, Maharajah Ganga, 55
Singh, Sarina, 3

Singapore airport, 86
*Social Research,* 22
Statistics:
  India, 7-8
  Rajasthan, 8
  world tourism, 7
*Strange Lands and Friendly People,* 60-61
*Suitable Boy,* 81
*Sunday Times of India,* 74-75

Taj Mahal, 5, 44, 48, 50-52, 72
Tata steel company, 58
Thar Desert:
  camel ride near Bikaner, 88-89
Thompson, Michael, 32-33
*Time* magazine, 44, 96
Tourism:
  expenditures by countries, 7
  problems tourists face, 45-46
  stages involved in, 43-45
  statistics for European countries
  Vietnam and Thailand, 4
*Tourist: A New Theory of the Leisure Class,* 41
Tourists:
  search for authenticity, 84
  stages in a trip, 81-85
*Travel & Leisure,* 96
*Tristes Tropiques,* 9
Turkey, 11

UNESCO World Heritage Site, 52, 71
*US News & World Report,* 96
Uttar Pradesh, 61, 95

*Wall Street Journal,* 9, 96
Weber, Max, 20
Wildvasky, Aaron, 31-33
*World Food India,* 81
World Tourist Organization, 6

Zeman, J. Jay, 42, 43

For Product Safety Concerns and Information please contact our EU
representative GPSR@taylorandfrancis.com
Taylor & Francis Verlag GmbH, Kaufingerstraße 24, 80331 München, Germany

www.ingramcontent.com/pod-product-compliance
Lightning Source LLC
Chambersburg PA
CBHW070629300426
44113CB00010B/1716